PERSPICACITY

PERSPICACITY

MARTIN LEONARD GARDNER

authorHOUSE®

AuthorHouse™
1663 Liberty Drive
Bloomington, IN 47403
www.authorhouse.com
Phone: 1-800-839-8640

Published by AuthorHouse   10/19/2012

ISBN: 978-1-4772-8056-0 (sc)
ISBN: 978-1-4772-8054-6 (hc)
ISBN: 978-1-4772-8055-3 (e)

Library of Congress Control Number: 2012919698

Contents

"You can't solve a problem with the same mind and thinking that created the problem in the first place."

—Albert Einstein

Preface

Perspicacious: Having keen mental perception or discernment. Perhaps in simple terms, *awareness.*

Discernment: Acuteness of judgment; the power to perceive differences between things or ideas, as well as their relationships.

The above definitions, taken from *The Living Webster Encyclopedic Dictionary of the English Language,* are there to help readers understand that this book is not a panacea of definite fact to be construed to hold irrefutable information; instead it is a book that expresses opinion based on how the author perceives these issues to be. In other words, these are opinions expressed by the common, ordinary, everyday person with a passion to let out that which needs to be said.

Subjects within this book are not necessarily political, although they can be construed as such. The author is annoyed with what is happening to the people of this country because he sees that which he feels is inevitable.

In the year 2000, the very second George W. Bush was appointed by the Supreme Court to be the forty-third president of the United States, the author stated openly, "We will be at war within two years with Iraq." This was only one of many predictions—but the most outstanding—where the author was absolutely correct. I am not a prognosticator by profession, but to me this was just too obvious, given the attempt on the life of his father and the body language displayed by him.

Too few have too much power in this country, and I think you all know what history has taught us as respects that issue. I am not a religious person, yet I fear that which is in the bible predicting Armageddon. We seem to be headed in that direction, and I do not think the world will awaken soon enough to prevent it.

My greatest hope is that some of this book may turn some things around and thus begin a snowball effect to turn the world around for the better. This nation has, within its power, the ability to turn itself around, and from a position of strength, not power, turn the rest of the world around also.

Do we have the time?

Traffic Rules

I often wonder how many of us fully understand the whys and wherefores of some of the wonderful traffic laws we have placed in force. For example, someone realized that it would save a lot of energy and time if we allowed drivers the opportunity, after coming to a complete stop, to make a right turn on a red light. Of course, the idea was that they had to first yield right of way to any oncoming cars. Subsequent to that, someone thought of the green arrow, which gave exclusivity for making a right or left turn, so that drivers didn't have to yield to anyone, nor were they required to stop before turning. Brilliant so far, right? Then came the blinking red arrow, which allowed the driver the opportunity of turning—but only after making a full stop and yielding right of way to any oncoming cars. Somehow, I was under the impression that the red light did that! The solid red arrow meant you couldn't, under any circumstances, enter the intersection until the light turned green. The blinking yellow arrow allowed you to turn, however you had to use caution for possible oncoming cars. Stopping wasn't a requirement unless there was someone for whom you must yield right of way. Now comes the green arrow, which allows you to make a U-turn. Of course, the green arrow means you have exclusive rights to the intersection and can make your U-turn at will. Or can you? It seems that they threw another zinger into the equation with a sign that says "U-Turning vehicles must yield right of way." Now let's see what that means! You are making a U-turn on a green arrow, and you must yield right of way to the car making a right turn on a red light who is supposed to yield right of way to anyone in that

4

intersection. Clear as mud, right? Now let's add salt to the wound because invariably there is a pedestrian or bicycle rider that you cannot see because you are looking for that car that has the right of way. Still think taking the bus is not such a good idea? If you are turning right on a red light, you are looking to the left to see if there are any cars coming your way. Seeing that pedestrian step off the sidewalk to your right is almost impossible.

Now let's look at an accident waiting to happen; this intersection actually exists in Port Saint Lucie, Florida, at Airoso and Saint James. Please note that there are only two lanes coming into this dilemma, which turns into three lanes as the right lane becomes a right-turn-only lane. Now, the auto in the middle, which is really the left lane, can either move to the left or go straight, but the car in the right wishing to get into the middle lane, not wishing to make a right turn, must wait until the car in the middle goes to the left or there will be an accident, especially if the car in the left is behind him and doesn't see him coming, or if there are multiple cars in that lane. The car in the left lane has a choice! This is the problem, as he can either stay in the right lane, which happens to be the middle lane now, or he can go over to the left lane. He should not have that choice; it should be mandatory for him to turn into the left lane. That could be done by a solid line directing him to that lane. He is in the left lane and should remain there unless he decides to change lanes—and that can only be done if there is not an oncoming car in that lane.

Sound confusing? Really it is not. You must maintain the belief that there are really only two lanes, but you must consider the right lane, which should not become a right-turn-only lane all of a sudden. If you consider that the right lane lines should swing over to the left lane, which now becomes the middle lane while the left lane remains the left lane, then all will work. If the auto in the left lane is forced to remain in the left lane, then the right lane has the option of being either the middle lane or the right lane, which is the right-turn-only lane.

Airoso Blvd.

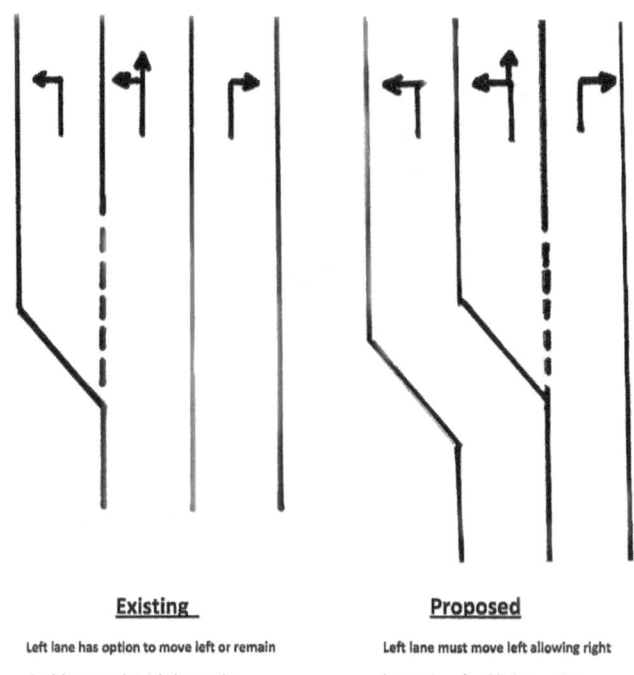

Existing	Proposed
Left lane has option to move left or remain Straight preventing right lane option.	Left lane must move left allowing right lane option of middle lane vs. R turn

Same intersection coming from Airoso Blvd onto Saint James.

Please note that there is a *green arrow* on a small island telling you that you may proceed safely. That light burns 24/7. Why? You tell me! It is a waste of electrical energy. I have no idea how much it cost to install that light, but even if it cost $1.00, though I am sure it was thousands, it is still a waste of *tax payers'* money and is costing the taxpayers every day. If the traffic controller was only interested in telling you that you can turn with confidence, how about a reflecting sign telling you that or at the very least, a *yield* sign.

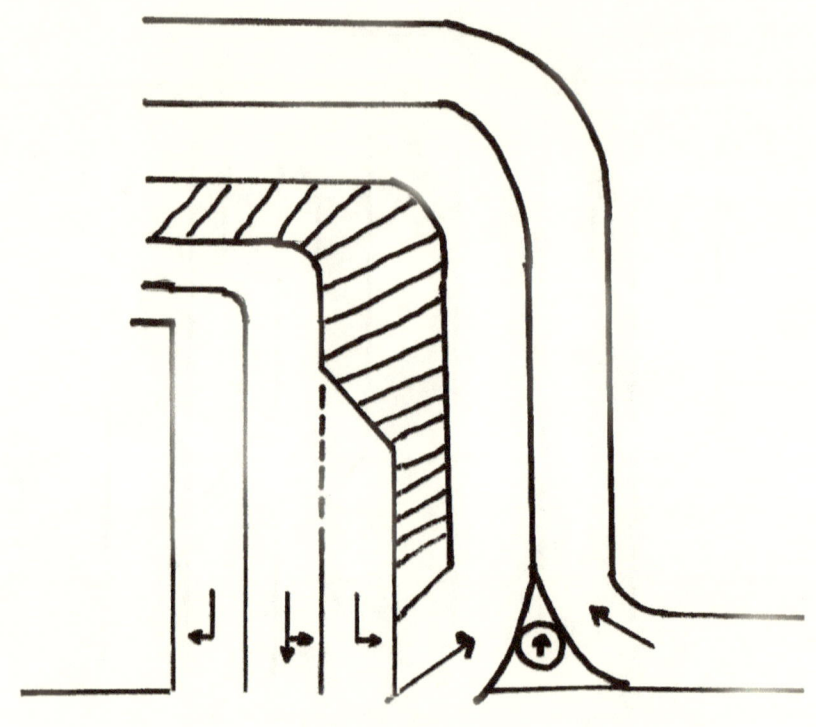

Airoso Blvd.

Traffic lights: When you are traveling along a major road, somehow you always seem to be looking up at the oncoming traffic light and hoping that it stays green long enough for you to be under it. Have you ever noticed that you are dreaming? They always turn yellow just at the point that you cannot go through and therefore must stop. Try telling the cop that the light turned as you entered the intersection so you put the car in passing gear in order to avoid wasting gasoline! The traffic lights are a conspiracy. They waste fuel and always work in the opposite direction so you catch every single one of them. The best way to avoid getting caught by the lights is to go eight miles an hour over the speed limit. Now you are traveling fast enough to beat the system—until you get pulled over by the bubble gum machine that has been following you for the last three miles, clocking your speed. Cops don't need a reason to pull you over and give you a ticket. The road rules are confusing enough that you don't have a chance, and if you don't believe that, reread the first paragraph in this chapter. There is a newly constructed road, known as Cross Town Parkway, that goes over I-95. If you are entering I-95, you will almost always get stopped by the traffic light. When the light lets you go over the bridge, you will definitely get stopped by the next light and have to wait to enter I-95. You cannot win because the traffic control experts are not that at all; they are just people working for the city who know not what they do.

This town of Port Saint Lucie, Florida is just a tiny town on the map, but if I can find all these errors, imagine what you can find all over this great nation. Just to prove a point, let us look upon

another brilliant accomplishment of engineering. Above is a picture of the Cross Town Parkway where, at the end, the road swings to the left and you are guided by a six-inch curb that guides you to swing to the left. Mind you now, there is no intersection. However, if you look just befor the road turns to the left, there are two stop signs that serve absolutely no purpose except to give the police a place to issue tickets, and, according to some of the natives, many a ticket was in fact issued there.

Now I want you to notice that the road ends but continues, as you can only turn left to follow the road. There is absolutely no way another car can have right of way, but you are required to stop for, you guessed it, no one. These inordinate stop signs serve absolutely no constructive purpose. Please note there are curbs that go all the way around the turn, making it almost impossible to go any other direction. This is not an intersection; it is a continuation of a road. Imagine, if you will, a stop sign on the interstate because it bears to the left, and you have the same logic. Now brace yourself, because you know what is coming next. The traffic coming from the other side, entering this turn to go the opposite direction, also has a stop sign to protect the turners from, once again, you guessed it: no one.

Intelligent!

United States Energy Policy

In this day and age of sophistication and education reliance, I find it hard to believe we cannot see the forest, for the trees are blocking our view. Perhaps it is this great religious belief that God will take care of us. That God won't let us do the wrong thing. After all, we must all realize that God talked to G. W. Bush, and his decision to invade Iraq had to be correct for that reason.

I am a good one for stating the inevitable. It is an undeniable fact that for every action, there is an equal and opposite reaction. Having said that, perhaps you will allow me the theory that, in my opinion, will lead to the destruction of this planet.

In the beginning, man was placed on this planet as a being from a distant world! Wow! Now that sounds farfetched, as we all know that God created Adam, and Eve came from one of his ribs. Eve had two sons, and those sons took wives. God said, "Go forth and be fruitful."

Now that is as logical as asking why the sky is blue. Because God made it that way! Where did the wives come from? No one asks that question!

There are many such fairy tales in the Bible, but that is not why I am writing this book. I would like to express my theory and see where it leads us. As I said, for every action there is an equal and opposite reaction. Black gold, as it is often referred to, is hydraulic fluid that fills in the imperfections of the structure of our planet. Keep on removing that hydraulic fluid, and this planet we inhabit will collapse. As it loses its shape, we will be thrown out of orbit, and at that point will come the destruction I spoke of before. It has already begun with landslides in Canada just recently, increases of earthquakes throughout the world, droughts, floods, hurricanes, fires, tornados, and hostilities among nations brought on by economics and religion. As a result of these phenomena—worldwide hunger and starvation.

The latest edition of the movie "The Day the Earth Stood Still" had more meaning than most people have thought about. When Klaatu, the visitor from outer space, spoke of saving the Earth, he also indicated, *from us*. Now, does that give you an indication that there is an undermining intent to let us know that we are destroying our planet? He made mention that "there are only a handful of planets in the cosmos capable of supporting complex life" and the group of civilizations, which he represents, is of the impression that this is one of those planets. He made specific reference: "If the Earth dies, you die! If you die, the Earth has a chance to heal itself."

Now, let's get back to my theory that man was placed upon this planet by beings of another world. You can believe what you want, but when you consider that the Great Pyramids were built of granite stones, which there is no way even today to build with, stones brought there riding on logs, when there were no hardwood trees in that region, with a triangular top, though there is no way man could leverage it to place it on top of the structure. Blocks placed perfectly in place, which we have no way of moving and hallways with rooms running throughout. It would certainly sound more logical to say that superior beings with technology we haven't even begun to explore built those pyramids, rather than saying that thousands of slaves along with mathematical leverages moved those blocks from the Nile across the desert on logs that do not exist, across the burning sands without roads to support the logs. Man was seeded here because a former civilization that destroyed their world did the same thing we are doing to this planet.

"Drill baby, drill," and expect the same results. You cannot expect to do the same thing over and over and get different results! To put it plainly, we are destroying this planet, and the final analysis will not differ. We must use our technology to create energy and do all we can to coexist with this planet or, because of money, we will be writing our epitaph: "Money is the root of all evil!"

Why are we still using fossil fuels to create the energy we need when there are so many other resources that are reusable sources? All these years, we have been taking the hydraulic fluids out of the earth, the number of barrels staggering to the imagination. Why are we not building monorails throughout this great nation to move the people magnetically instead of using fossil fuels that eventually will run out anyway? People don't want to use the electric car because their distance of travel will be cut short. Why is this being told to the people? Motors, not engines, are capable of turning generators which, by the way, are almost identical to one another, which in turn can charge batteries that keep the motors running. I know, I know! That would kind of disprove the theory of perpetual motion. That is not the case, as all parts have a lifespan and would need to be replaced, just like the internal combustion engine that pollutes our atmosphere. If monorails were built throughout the nation, there would be no need for long-distance driving. Only a drive to the monorail to be picked up by an electric bus from the monorail and delivered to the final destination. The return would be exactly the opposite.

Talk about creating employment; I am not so sure we have enough people to fill the jobs. Infrastructure would have to be created (construction). Systems would have to be created on the drawing boards (engineering). Actual structures to mount the monorail cars, not to mention the cars themselves. Electrical conduits manufactured installed and monitored. Computer systems to run the systems safely. Energy sources to run the system, including nuclear as well as solar and wind and perhaps even use of the ever-moving oceans, which, by the way, happen to be in perpetual motion. Now let's talk about a pipeline from Canada to transport more of that hydraulic fluid that must be refined in those refineries that are outdated and couldn't handle the job anyway. How much of that fuel would be consumed here in this country vs. sold to other countries, with the American people footing the bill and the profits going to such companies as Exxon/ Mobile, etc.?

This country was made great by uniting all the states in building a railroad that moves everything we need from one place to another. We have built dams and cut through mountains. We have built skyscrapers and subway tunnels. Everything we need comes from somewhere and is brought to us by ships, rails, trucks, and sometimes even planes. All this comes from a system known as *capitalism*! We cannot allow this system to rule this country, so we temper it with *socialism*! Now, I know there are those who think socialism means communism and being progressive is a bad thing, but very few discern that a complex society such as this one needs a system of *checks and balances,* which is what is needed to maintain a peaceful coexistence.

Change is always necessary, as we live in a technological world. Perhaps those that hate progressives aren't so against change as they indicate. If we could only stop bickering among ourselves as to which forms of government we want, accept the fact that we need to govern ourselves, know that to be part of that governing is an honor and not a career to be paid the rest of their lives, along with benefits. Perhaps this country can become great again, if we have the time, as the damage might not be repairable when you consider all the years we have been raping Mother Nature. Will Klaatu give us the time to change and do we have the will to change? What is the alternative? What will money be worth if the Earth is no longer?

The Future of This Country!

I don't know about you, but it seems that we are in a real pickle as respects our youth. Please don't forget: the future is in their hands, and how bright that future may appear to you doesn't matter. What does matter is what you do with it. It seems we are more interested in raping our natural resources, growing our ambitions, and making certain we take as big of a bite out of the apple as possible without regard to perpetuation of our way of life. Whatever happened to:

We The People?

It seems to me that phrase has gone by the wayside and has been replaced with:

I got mine!

We have a new breed of leader who tells us all what God wants us to do while they start out with a salary of $174,000 and in a few short years become multimillionaires. Doesn't anyone out there see the truth? *Doesn't anyone out there care?*

I, for one, am sick of it, and that is why I am writing this book, which I hope will be read by some of you who can still read. It certainly appears as if we would rather curl up in front of the boob tube and take in all the lies that are being told to us. I have noticed more and more that people are being brainwashed.

Don't you see what is going on? Every time a politician gets another law passed, we lose another freedom. They are taking our freedom away, and we are like cows and are just giving it up. The Internet is just filled with statements that are not true, but no one bothers to check them out by going to Snopes.com or Wikipedia, for example. They just take in the information (propaganda) and will defend that bunch of lies to the destruction of their friendships and families. I get a kick out of some of the garbage I receive from some of my friends, all in a lather for no reason—when all they had to do was check into the validity of the statement. Let me give you something to think about. We have children, and we raise them as best we can, but even though we place them in the best surroundings we can afford, it seems the drug people get to them. Why is that? Simple answer but you will have to do some actual reading to get it. We perpetuate the bad and disregard the needed. Have you ever noticed how large the prisons budget has gotten? Have you taken notice that there is a reason? Let me explain it to you, because this is the greatest sales job ever in the history of mankind.

Endless Entanglement

Please, just imagine for a moment that you are a young child, around the age of fourteen. You are going to school, like any other child, and, like most, you are getting by, by the skin of your teeth. It doesn't matter if you are a boy or girl, as sex plays no part in this scenario. One of your concerns is that you want to be popular, or at least accepted by your peers. Perhaps you have a learning disability that the school system refuses to recognize and you are having a tough time getting through. Your folks care, but you cannot appreciate their plight, as you are too busy being concerned with your own.

One day, someone, vaguely familiar to you, suddenly becomes your friend, and, because you are confused, you begin to confide your feelings to this person. You are not a bad person; as a matter of fact, you are well-mannered and polite. You form a relationship with this person, and, without realizing it, suddenly you are a victim of the world of drugs. It starts off slowly but gets progressive as time goes on. Your parents notice a change of personality and, in their concern, begin questioning you. In your confusion, you mistake their action as manipulative and intrusive, thereby shutting out the only people truly concerned about your welfare. You begin lying and subsequently stealing in an effort to support your newfound habit. At the beginning, you are stealing from your family and friends' families, but as the need for more of these drugs becomes more prevalent, you begin to realize that you haven't the capability to pay for the drugs. In an effort to satisfy your hunger for drugs and to keep from becoming sick, nauseous, sweating, and suicidal, you will do anything. Your newfound friend tells you that you could get all the drugs you want—if you get more people into the system. As a result of your needs, you drop out of school because your friend tells you that you can always get a GED later on. Since you are a person of the world, you agree.

I am in the sales business and have always been against multilevel marketing. This is an example of such in the worst way, as this instance is *illegal*. Not multilevel marketing but the particular product that is being sold is illegal.

You are now advancing an illegal business—and not for profit, but to keep yourself supplied with the product to satisfy your own needs. Now you have many friends doing the same thing you have been doing to keep themselves in the product, and they develop many friends, and so on, and so forth. You begin to make money with your newfound business and you begin moving up the ladder. If you are lucky, you get high enough up the ladder that you become important to those that have the resources to hire the best attorneys when you get caught by the authorities so that you get off the hook.

The Spider and the Fly

This story is not about that person but a fly that is not so lucky as to get high enough up the ladder. This fly gets caught by a spider sitting in its web and saying, "Come into my house."

Now, it wouldn't be so bad if this spider arrested this fly, that is now of age, and the courts sent this fly off to rehab with hopes of being rehabilitated. But no! This fly is given a slap on the wrist and turned back out into society after being told not to do it again. The fly is on probation for whatever length of time the crime merits.

The spider, of course, only turned in sufficient evidence to convict the fly—and kept the balance for personal consumption or sale with impunity, as the fly couldn't tell the truth for fear of self-incrimination. The fly, turned out into the world again in need of more of the product, continues to perform illegal activities until it is caught again.

Now, here is the stupid part of the story. The spider arrests the fly for trafficking and, once again, only turns in sufficient quantities to convict the fly. Well, you know the rest, but the fly, being convicted of this nonviolent crime, is finally sent off to rehab and given the title of *felon*. After being held in jail for whatever time needed to set up the rehab, the fly gets to meet other flies. After spending whatever time necessary in jail, the fly goes off to rehabilitation and spends perhaps a year. The rehab center just happens to be in the middle of crack town, and more drugs are going through that rehab center than you could ever imagine. More contacts are being made and the potential for more multilevel marketing is increased exponentially.

The fly gets out after the predetermined time and is supposed to be cured from its habit (disease). The then-cured fly who wants nothing more to do with drugs now must fit into society by getting a job. Ah! Now therein lies the key! After filling out many applications and being turned down because the fly is now a felon, the fly has no choice but to return to its previous life of crime, as, unfortunately, the fly has another habit that is unbreakable and that is the need to eat. The fly gets caught again by a spider and goes to prison. The same scenario repeats, and thus the prisons are overloaded and, of course, perpetuated.

The preceding is mostly a true reenactment, but the truth is that our system is failing us, and it will only get worse until we decide to fix it. The lack of perspicacity within our system startles me, and I am just one person. I wonder how many others realize it and if anything can be done about it in time to prevent total collapse, as these drugs will destroy us all. Continuing on the same path will only perpetuate the same results. We must get some judges with intelligence enough to break the cycle, and we must go after the big guys. If we stop the source, we can stop the fly—but stopping the fly will only amount to more flies. Branding someone with the title *felon* is the most irresponsible act any judge can do. A nonviolent crime is not one against society but a self-incriminating act that our system perpetuates, and it must be stopped.

Isn't it wonderful that we take the victims and turn them into criminals who take other children into the fold—and the multilevel marketing grows bigger and bigger while the real problem lies in the prison lobbies.

The prisons are just filled with people that have committed nonviolent crimes. People who were dangerous only to themselves. A system that is perpetuated by the courts, which seem to perpetuate their own existence. Our legal system is mostly to blame, as it punishes the victims instead of the perpetrators. A disease should be treated by medical people, not prison guards! Let's not go after the fly! Let's get the queen, and the flies will come to an end. You want to save the world? Start here by being perspicacious. Putting your head in the sand only accomplishes one thing: getting sand in your nose and ears. *Perspicacity is the key!*

It never ceases to amaze me that we can go to war against people we never should have attacked. We can go to a disaster anywhere in the world to give aid. We can send probes through space to gather information, which we can do nothing about. We can build a space station with cooperation of other countries. We can locate and define causes for problems such as the Titanic sinking in waters no man could tolerate. We can treat most diseases—notice I said treat, because it is too obvious we do not want to cure, for it is not economically feasible. But we cannot stop sopping the hydraulic fluid that holds the earth's shape, as habits are economically incurable. We have people who say all the world's scientists do not know what they are talking about when they recognize that global warming exists, and if we continue on the same path, we will destroy our planet. Why aren't we smart enough to know that the victims are not the ones we need to punish? If we fix the victims, there won't be such a need for prisons, and perhaps we could have enough funds to fix the other problems that are pressing, like saving the Earth.

When are the judges going to wake up and see that these kids aren't criminals? When are they going to realize they are victims, and the sooner we induct them into the business world, the sooner we can keep them busy enough to keep off of drugs. When are they going to wake up and see that the money should be put into the school system, and, if that were the case, we wouldn't need so many prisons, and people such as the person above who has a learning disability will have funds to recognize the problem and work with it.

Now that we realize the money is going in the wrong direction, how can we change that? You know, I find it hard to believe that 1 percent of the nation owns 95 percent of its wealth. There has to be an explanation. You go to work eight hours and I go to work eight hours, but I make $100,000 an hour doing very little, and you make $15 per hour busting your ass. You know, that is the capitalistic society and you can complain about it all you want, it is still the best society in the world.

Mark Zuckerberg has become a very wealthy man, and no one gave it to him. He *happened* to be in the right place at the right time with the right idea—and that could happen to anyone. It doesn't matter what your education is, your skill, or the talent you possess. Some of us will make it, and most of us will not. What is important, though, is that all have the same opportunity. What is also important is those who make it do their best to create opportunities for others so that this country grows and perpetuates the capitalistic society. There will always be those who want everything handed to them, but they can remain dreamers forever. What is hopeful is that the haves will create opportunities for the have-nots to grow and perhaps become haves. Let's take a look at the preamble to the Constitution which states the following:

We the people of the United States in order to form a more perfect union, establish justice, insure domestic tranquility, provide for the common defense, promote the general welfare and secure the blessings of liberty to ourselves and our posterity, do ordain and establish this constitution for the United States of America.

For those of you that are not familiar with the term posterity, let me spread a little perspicacity. It means: our offspring, our children, the next generation.

While it is important for us to create a condition of advantage for our children, it is just as important to spread liberty throughout the land. Those who have, also have the obligation to make this a better world, because without the people, your posterity will have no meaning. Use some of that bite you have taken out of the apple. The government should not have to take it; nor should the people. Be a little more caring. Use your wealth to create more wealth by creating jobs. Just sitting on money only makes it stale. Make it work! This nation needs a monorail system to get us off of the fossil fuel and become more energy efficient. We need to educate our young so the next generation of engineers and doctors are ready for the task of being the greatest nation on earth.

As the Platters sang, "Only you can make all our dreams come true!"

Fulton made the steam engine a reality. Private enterprise built the railroads, and because of them, this nation became a wonderful nation worth fighting for—and please don't ever forget that it was the common people who fought and died to give to you this great nation. I implore you to make us great again. We have the greatest workers in the world here in this country. Give them something to build, and watch this country rise up to be the model for the rest of the world. The challenge is enormous, and the rewards are a legacy. Despite the fact that the rest of the world hates us or at the very least is envious of us, we must realize that to straighten out our country first is with certainty our first priority. When we are straightened out and the rest of the world sees this, then and only then do we have the prestige to help the rest of the world. If you need proof of that, just look at the present circumstances. The 1 percent are people, capitalists, who realize that building factories where ecology rules do not apply certainly would bring more profit. Building where labor is much cheaper adds to the bottom line. Using labor that doesn't require benefits such as health insurance, pensions, paid holidays, and working conditions controlled by law saves money. All this is in the name of capitalism—and, although I cannot condemn this action, I must also realize there is a factor known as the *pendulum*. This is a device that swings only so far before it must return to the opposite direction, passing the center and swinging again in the opposite direction. The 1 percent never thought about the fact that to depreciate the buying power of the American worker would only have a destructive, adverse impact on their endeavor. For each action, there is an equal and opposite reaction. Look at the rest of the world, and notice that they are crumbling. You must have compassion for these people, but first and foremost, we must repair our economy. We have the resources necessary, and all we need is the will. The people have the will but not the resources. We cannot wait for this twisted, non-committal, and political government to make a move to improve this country. When politics becomes more important than the welfare of the country, it is time to take the bull by the horns. Free enterprise is and always has been the key to our greatness. Free enterprise is our goal, and free enterprise will and must prevail. If the 1 percent wants to feel the security of knowing that they live in the free society protected by law which is defended by the people, let's roll up our sleeves and get to work to rebuild this great nation, our economy, and our prestige. A symbiosis must penetrate the dysfunctional Washington D. C. and *we, the people* must, once again, prove that a peaceful solution to a nation's strife can and does prevail. Perhaps that is the only way to gain respect and have others look up to our way of life and emulate it instead of despising it.

Let me leave those movers of the factories some food for thought. You are encroaching on land for which you are not protected by the Constitution of the United States. Today, these countries may honor patents, but that could change at any moment and your investment could be lost forever.

Laws, Rules, and the Enforcers

For those uninformed people, the word "cop" was a contraction from the original badge which was made out of copper. The police officer was originally supposed to be a *peace officer,* and the laws were supposed to protect the people. It appears as if the police have become the genuine agitators of the people. The laws have been twisted to protect the guilty, and the courts have turned out to be a battleground for which justice seems to be a long forgotten word.

Justice: Equitableness; unprejudiced adjudication of conflicting interest on the basis of legal or moral principles; lawfulness; what is rightly due.

Verdict: The answer of a jury given to the court concerning any matter committed to their examination and judgment. A decision, judgment or opinion. Perhaps better described in the movie, My Cousin Vinnie, as "truth."

The courtroom today is a battleground between the prosecutor and the defense, and anything used to win is fair game. *Win* is the key word here. It has become more important to win your point than to determine the truth. It matters not that perspicacity of fallacious, malicious evidence is thrown into the equation; it matters not that exculpatory evidence is hidden from the courts and the defense. All that matters is putting another notch on the prosecutor's gun. That was not the intent of our legal system. The judges and the prosecutors are not incongruent, and as a result, there are many in prison who are innocent. It is a presumption that if the person is of a certain persuasion, he is guilty as charged. The poor are offered a public defender that has a caseload big enough for a staff of attorneys, while the rich hire staffs of attorneys and remain untouchable. Right or wrong is not the question here; how much money do you have is. The percentage of minority people in prison vs. upper-income to wealthy is mind-boggling. The manufacture of evidence is not outside the ethics boundaries, as we have seen in the OJ Simpson trial. Remember, the sock that wasn't there and suddenly was there, that had blood on both sides of the ankle? The soaking wet glove, wet with blood that didn't even have a blade of grass stuck on it, found on the lawn next to the air conditioning pad? The Bronco driven by an officer of the court to the impound section who initially said there was no blood, but suddenly there was blood all over its interior? The vials of OJ's blood found in the desk of the chief investigator?

Had the evidence fallen as it was, perhaps the verdict might have been different, but to make the case stronger, evidence had to be manufactured. I am happy to say the jury saw otherwise. I am not saying that OJ was innocent, and I am not saying he was guilty, but truth was not served here, and the same holds true in most courtrooms. Whether he was guilty or innocent is irrelevant! What is relevant is that, based on what was shown to the jury, I would have given a verdict as innocent a result of manufactured evidence from the prosecution.

Many judges are elected, and many are appointed. Most start out with the right idea of exactly what justice is, with the correct ethical background and desire to do the right job. Notice I said *most*! I brought that thought up as, most in a pragmatic way, try to do what is right, but something interferes with that process. By doing the same thing over and over again, each case runs into the next case, and soon all seem so much alike that perspective is lost. They lose the ability to be compassionate and thus lose the ability to differentiate truth from fiction. You see, in this wonderful nation of ours, a person is presumed innocent until *proven guilty*! That, my friends, is the *law of the land*! That, my friends, is what is missing!

Now, I am not a judge, jury, and executioner. I am merely a person with perspicacity that is expressing his opinion based on facts as I perceive them to be.

1969, in Suffolk County, New York, Dix Hills, there is a road, I do not remember the name of, that runs alongside a housing community. A winding, hilly road where people know they must be cautious of their speed. I was entering that road, making a left turn. To do this task, I first had to stop at the stop sign and make a few more stops to be certain I had room to make that turn, as visibility was impeded by a hill. I began to enter when, out of the blue, a car came over the hill bearing down on me so fast it took him about half a football field to stop. If that car were within the speed limit, stopping certainly would not have been a problem. Had my reflexes been a little slow, I would not be writing this book today. That car was a police car whose driver was completely wrong but gave me a ticket. This is not what I am getting at, so please bear with me for a moment. Knowing I was not wrong, I took pictures of the area and the skid marks the police car had made, and I went to court. I listened to case after case where the officers gave speeding tickets to drivers based on the fact that their eyes were checked out. You got that? Their eyes were checked out to tell speed! Of course, the judge backed those tickets, so the cop lied and the judge swore to it. I knew I was in a kangaroo court. Enough said???

When the police forget they are supposed to be peace officers, to keep the peace and protect the innocent, not harass them; when the court system learns they are there to make judgments for the truth, that laws are made to protect the innocent, not incarcerate them, we can then make true claim that this is the land of the free. The old expression, "The truth will set you free," is, in the system as it is today, as false as a pot of gold at the end of the rainbow.

Our prison system is overcrowded, as too many innocent people are behind bars. This has been proven over and over again by DNA tests that tell us our system is corrupt. Once again let me say, "You are innocent until *proven* guilty." Our system has failed because our judges have failed, and the police are too inventive, and they are backed by the prosecutor, who is backed by the judge of ill competence.

We don't ask for much, just a justice system that is what it claims to be—but should it decide to continue as it is now we might as well call it the Gestapo system of no justice.

The Supreme Court's only function is to determine constitutionality of laws. As I see it, today it is the final judgment place of telling you how to run your lives and what morals you must have, based on the religious morals of the judges sitting on the bench.

How do you like being told whether or not you can have an abortion, who or what you are allowed to marry, what is good and what is bad for your health? Marijuana is not legal but alcohol is! It seems both can screw up your brain and impede your judgment, while only one is used as a treatment for certain diseases and the other, well, I think you get the picture. I often wonder how many deaths are from driving under the influence of marijuana as opposed to legal drugs or alcohol. How many diseases STDs could be prevented had we allowed prostitutes to be in business—but under the control of the medical profession? How much revenue could be gained by taxing such a service? I often wonder why we make such an industry illegal. Has making it illegal prevented the profession from existence?

I think it is about time we grew up and began making decisions of our own, so long as it doesn't impede the rights of others. We hire politicians to work for us, not the other way around. I think it is about time we started telling them what we want instead of them telling us what they want. We want laws that make sense and written in such language that we can all interpret. We speak English, not Latin! Simplify the law, and make it fit every circumstance and class of individual, not just for some. Get rid of antiquated laws that do not apply such as, it is illegal for a man to kiss his wife on Sunday. When I go to court, I want the judge to speak to me in English so I can understand what is being said about me. In most cases, I shouldn't need an attorney to defend the confusion created by the way the charges are being handed down to me. If I am guilty of a crime, I'll know it myself, and if I committed a crime, I must be ready to pay the consequence—but if I am innocent of such a crime, I should not be unjustly prosecuted and confused into admission of that crime.

Isn't it wonderful that they give to you the privilege of electing many of the judges that sit on the stand in judgment of you? My, my, my! You get a name, and they expect you to vote on that basis. Did anyone ever get a history of any of these judges before voting? Do any of you know what that person stands for? You get what you ask for. He is a nice young Italian or a Jew or a Black, or she is a good-looking woman. Kind of like voting for the tax collector! Why don't they at least give a history of what each person stands for as well as a history of past decisions? I don't think people are voting responsibly because if they were, we might have better choices.

How about a woman judge that refuses to recognize, within the county, drug rehabilitation facilities, who sends people she convicts to a drug rehabilitation about 100 miles away in Miami, where a young man died from pneumonia because the administration refused to give him his medication. Why won't she send them to a local, highly reputable rehabilitation center right in their own backyard? Don't you think the people deserve better?

We hold judges in high esteem, expecting them to be unbiased and have enough knowledge of the law that they can sift out the truth. There are always three sides to every story! Yours, mine, and somewhere therein lies the truth. When you are a judge, it is your duty to sift out the truth! I witnessed a judge sitting on the bench, not really listening to the convicted individual. I knew, just watching him, it didn't matter what the person had to say, he was going to stay firm on his preconceived notion.

The story, as I have been told, and I did not see the records, is a women knew a man for six days when he asked her to drive him from point "A" to point "B," which is what she agreed to do. She was pulled over by a police officer and charged with accessory to murder. Somehow, the logic escapes me, especially since she had absolutely no prior record of ever breaking the law. If what I had heard is true, don't you think the judge should have looked further into such a case? How many people are incarcerated just to keep the prison lobby people happy? I truly wonder!

History of the National Debt

I find it very disturbing that politicians use the national debt as a political football. We have had national debt since the founding of this country. In 1791, during the American Revolutionary War, under the Articles of Confederation, the national debt totaled $75,463,476.52. Between 1796 and 1811, there were fourteen surplus years and two deficit years, and then came the War of 1812, which brought about a sharp increase in the national debt.

Following that war, there were eighteen years of surplus, and at the end of twenty years, the U. S. paid off 99.97 percent of its then debt.

The Civil War, 1861-1865, brought about another sharp increase in the debt. The debt was just $65 million in 1860 but passed $1 billion in 1863 and reached $2.7 billion by the end of the war. Nice short wars, right?

The next forty-seven years brought about thirty-six surpluses and eleven deficits. During this time period, 55 percent of the national debt was paid off. At this point, it should be well understood that war brings about debt as, let's face it, wars are costly and must be paid for somehow. Please take note at the percentage of increase and throughout this article, notice that issue and please remember there were two wars created during the Bush administration.

World War I, 1914-1918, brought about the next sharp increase in the national debt, reaching $25.5 billion at its conclusion. Eleven consecutive surpluses brought about a reduction by 36 percent.

The Great Depression and World War II, during F. D. R. and the Truman presidencies in the 1930s and 1940s, caused the largest increase. The gross public debt increased sixteen times, from $16 billion in the 1930s to $260 billion in 1950. When Roosevelt took office in 1933, the national debt was almost $20 billion. By 1936, the national debt had increased to a mere $33.7 billion. Subsequently the gross debt was on the decline.

From 1965, the growth of the US aggregate debt began to increase quicker than GDP, as the GDP growth rates in Western countries began to taper off. The gross debt during the Regan and Bush presidencies, 1980-1992 quadrupled as a result of Reaganomics. Between 1992 and 2000, the numbers rose and fell from $3 trillion to $3.4 trillion, nothing to write home about right! President Clinton turned over what most would call a balanced budget.

Now comes George W. Bush, a president who inherited a balanced budget, and his first big decision was to give back to the people the surplus that Clinton had managed to save. Kind of like saying we are out of debt now so we need not save for a rainy day. The money belongs to the people, so let's make the slate even and give it back to stimulate the economy. Line 21 of your income tax return requested the amount you received, and if it just happened to put you in another income bracket, you lost a lot more than he gave to you—which you never asked for in the first place. Thus marks the first in a long list of ridiculous actions that broke this nation.

From January of 2001, the debt increased from $5.7 trillion to $10.7 trillion by February 2008. Keep in mind that an increase in debt has always been the norm during a war, and we were suddenly in two wars now, which were put on the country's credit card.

The end of the presidency of George W. Bush marked nothing short of economic calamity. Lehman Brothers went bankrupt. American International Group was about to go bankrupt, the entire U.S. auto industry was about to go under, the stock market was about to collapse, and the world economy was in a complete state of disarray. We were firmly entrenched in two wars we never should have been placed into, our factories had left the country, and unemployment rose at a rate that was out of control, not to mention Goldman Sachs, Fannie Mae and Freddie Mac.

Why anyone would want to jump onto Barak Obama and blame him for the current financial problems is beyond comprehension. Just using the national debt as an excuse to say his administration was the cause for all this is mind-boggling in this day and age. Let us remember one thing: if nothing else is to be made clear, the budget for the United States of America can only be *proposed* by the president. The House of Representatives must approve it, and they can write their own budget which they can approve even over the presidential veto.

One more thing! The entire industrialized world has socialized medicine—with exception of the United States of America. Strange that the excuse for wanting to crush it comes from the fact that we cannot afford it. We certainly couldn't afford two wars which we never should have gone into but that was okay.

"We Hold These Truths To Be Self-Evident"

Wow! That is a truism that seems to hold true in all cases and specifically in law that is the topic of this chapter. I am sure that you are aware that all laws are made to be broken—usually for the convenience of some attorney wishing to earn more than he or she is entitled to, without regard to the client and certainly without regard to the public at large. Let me give to you a specific example of a true settlement. This case is real, and I have the documents to prove it. Please note the main crux of this is to make sure that you are all made aware that not all attorneys are out to see that you are indemnified. By the way that term for insurance purposes is defined as follows: To indemnify is to place the person in the exact financial condition the person would have been had the loss not occurred, not a penny better or worse off. To simplify that, to make the person who has suffered the loss, whole!

Attorneys often talk about getting for you every penny you deserve. Now let's examine that. An employee of a company that did roofing fell off of a roof while performing his job, breaking his back in several places. This employee spent two years in what is known as a turtle shell. Pretty serious, don't you think? Please permit me to digress for a moment and advise of the facts of workers' compensation.

Workers' Compensation and Exclusive Remedy

Workers' compensation insurance stood for more than fifty years as the sole recourse of employees injured on the job. This exclusive remedy, embodied in workers' compensation statutes, was designed to provide injured employees with a schedule of benefits in exchange for their giving up the right to sue the employer. The statutes provided immunity to employers from common law actions brought by their employees for damages arising out of injuries received in the course of employment. Dual Capacity and Intentional Torts, none of which apply here, eroded this doctrine.

Third-Party-Over

The "third-party-over" doctrine used to breach the exclusive remedy concept involves the injured employee bringing suit against a third party who, for one reason or another, is able to bring an action against the employer. The employer then, who has paid workers compensation to his injured employee, faces the prospect of paying for the same injury based on the third-party suit.

Please stick with me just a little longer, and you will see the reasoning for this specific information, which I am sure you have no other need to know.

Courts that have allowed this occurrence have done so because the third-party action included a demand for contribution rather than indemnification (at a time when the Comprehensive General Liability exclusion applied only to indemnification). Earlier workers' compensation forms did not address this distinction. However, both the 1984 workers' compensation form and the 1986 CGL forms are worded so as to eliminate such a basis for third-party-over problems. FC&S/WC ER1

Now let me inform you of the dates we are speaking of here, which ran from January of 1996 through January of 1999. To my knowledge, every general liability policy has an exclusion to any workers' compensation related injury and will not respond where workers' compensation is responsible unless such loss exceeds the limits of coverage, which is usually $100,000 and will respond only under certain conditions as excess coverage, not primary coverage.

When an attorney takes on a workers' compensation case, he should first be knowledgeable of the subject, as this is a specialty field. He must also be aware that if the case goes to court, he will be awarded his fee in accordance with the courts and not what he wishes to establish such as in this case, 40 percent of the gross settlement. Either this attorney was not aware or he intentionally sued the general liability, which should never have responded, for personal gain and not for the benefit of his client. I leave the decision in your hands as to which took place.

Now let's look at the actual:

Final Distribution Closing Statement

Gross settlement proceeds	$110,000.00
Attorney's fees at 40 percent	$44,000.00

Costs Incurred: Itemized Cost $26,946.00
See copy of   Ledger Attached
                  (left out as not
                  necessary for this
                  illustration).

Gross balance to $39,053.48
client

Less: medical bills at your request:

The following providers of medical benefits have outstanding balances and will be paid directly.

1: Worker's Compensation Lien: $11,000.00
2: MD. (who shall remain anonymous): $1,060.00

Net proceeds to client after
payment of the above medical bills/liens: $26,993.48

Now that is what I call getting the client every penny he deserves! The client spent two years in a turtle shell and had continuous pain the rest of his life, which, by the way ended at age forty from a massive heart attack, leaving a widow with two children and an ex-wife with two children also. The workers' compensation award would have been very different in favor of the worker without the attorney, but that is conjecture on my part and should not have effect on your opinion. There was no wife at the time of the loss, as the worker was divorced from his first wife and had not yet met his second wife, or there would have been a third-party suit filed by the wife which would have meant more compensation for the attorney, grounds being lack of consortium.

In my opinion, I find this case despicable and a perfect case of greed and lack of professionalism. This lawyer should have been disbarred, but worse yet, the insurance company that paid the loss should have known better, while the workers' compensation carrier, knowing the case was their responsibility, should have been the company to respond. They sure were there when it came time to collect their $11,000 and the list of expenses listed by the attorney of $26,946.52 is so ambiguous my solid opinion is that it is, if you will pardon the expression, *Bullshit! Padded! A true case of thievery!* To put it bluntly, a case of greed over professionalism!

In the future I want you all to remember the following statement:

When you hear, "We want you to get every penny you deserve,"

Run like hell; you are about to get ripped off, so go to a public adjuster!

If the public adjuster needs a little help, he will enlist the services of an attorney or the services of the state insurance commissioner, and his expense list won't even exist.

The last thing anyone wants to do is consider there is justice for all, as nothing could be further from the truth. There is no uniformity within our courts, and I will give to you an example.

A young woman was a passenger in a pickup truck that was pulled over by the police using the probable or proximate cause that the rear tires appeared bald. The rear tires were like slicks but had quite a bit of tread on them. Seeing this in the dark of night would have been impossible, making the stop even more unbelievable thus inappropriate.

The fact is, the driver and the passenger were seen leaving the house that the sheriff was casing. The officer asked if the driver would mind if they searched the vehicle, to which the driver gave permission. That meant that it was now presumed the passenger could be searched, even though permission was not granted by the woman. For some unimaginable reason, the driver was never searched. A woman officer was called over to search the passenger, and drugs were found in her possession, as well as some prescriptions from a doctor's office. She was hiding them for the driver! The driver didn't even intervene, admitting the drugs were his, and to avoid arrest, he agreed to take the officers to the house where they received the prescriptions, admitting it was where he received them. Instead of doing a search of that house, where they would have found illegal drugs and an unauthorized prescription pad for which they now had probable cause to search, the passenger was brought up on charges of trafficking—not the driver—and the supplier was left free to disappear and set up business elsewhere.

Now I don't know about your feelings of this incident, but I believe the people who were supposedly trained to handle this type of incident completely botched this case. A guilty man and a supplier were both let off the hook, while an innocent woman went to jail and had a felony charge rammed down her throat by a judge, a charge that she will live with the rest of her life. A point of interest, there were OxyContin pills found in the passenger's possession, but they were conveniently never turned in. The only items that were turned in were those necessary for a conviction. That, however, is not where I want to go. The crux of this story came in the fact that the Judge set bail at $76,000 on a woman who couldn't rub two nickels together. In the next county, shortly thereafter, a man was brought up on charges of murder and bail was set at $50,000. I guess the legal system felt that the crime of drugs held more weight than murder. A woman with no ability to leave the country charged with trafficking, more than likely would do so then a wealthy man having the charge of murder. The police lied, and the judge swore to it and couldn't see through the fact that the vehicle should never have been stopped in the first place. Way to go!

I graduated high school in 1960. I spent the first two years of high school at one school and the last two years at another. I was fortunate enough to attend both senior proms. Both proms were held in the school gymnasium. Actually, there were many hops held in the school gymnasiums of both schools and most of the other schools throughout the country. If you fail to believe that, just watch *Grease*, a story of a typical high school at that same time. I find it disturbing that schools can no longer accommodate their students because of the possible lawsuits that most likely could ensue. Ah yes, what a wonderful legal system we have! People more interested in acquiring money by suing, as there is always a hungry attorney that convinces them of the fortune they stand to gain. Of course, money takes precedence over all, including a lifestyle for our children. Most senior proms today are played out at hotels which I know the students have no desire to be at. Right?

Question

Why is it that people refuse to take responsibility for their own actions or lack thereof? If we can get an attorney to be creative enough and convince the necessary people that the fault was a result of negligence on the part of someone else, when they know it was their own mistake, we can collect money. *Money*, the root of all evil! Just for an example, I have witnessed the following: A woman of excessive size and age walked into a grocery store and fell down. She claimed the floor was wet and that is the reason for her accident, from which her hip was broken. A common claim, for which collecting is made easy—but who is the intended victim? The floor wax man left the floor wet and never placed the appropriate signs marking the area. Good guess, but the floor wax man only did the striping, washing, and re-waxing in that particular store at 2:00 a.m. at the end of the month, and this accident happened three weeks later. The floor, by the way, wasn't even damp but it was shiny by a wax which was slip-proof and backed by Johnson & Johnson, with a $5 million insurance policy. The floor wax man always kept a diary, and the store also showed the billing, which further corroborated the report from the floor waxing man. The truth came later on, as the case progressed, that the woman broke her hip and fell, not the other way around—but money was the motivation for creating a case that never should have been brought up in the first place. Every time there is a false claim that is paid, please remember we all pay for that claim. Please, there are enough legitimate cases out there that should be paid for, don't create those that are not legitimate, as we are the bearers of the cost in the final analysis. Attorneys should be more investigative instead of salesmen in determining the validity of a case, and when there is validity, the amount of work merited should be determined by the courts and not a basis of settlement, as this leads only to greed overpowering righteousness.

I can recall an incident in which a man came into my office seeking minimal coverage for his automobile. I advised him that for me to write such a policy, I would need for him to write in his own hand the following:

"I am aware that PIP (Personal Injury Protection), which is all Florida law requires, will pay only for my medical and/or loss of income and will not defend me in the event of lawsuit."

He insisted, and I insisted he write that paragraph in his own hand, which he did. Now comes the accident, in which he had his boat trailer hitched to his car and he hit someone else. He went to an attorney to sue me on the basis of negligence by not giving him liability and property damage insurance along with the PIP. The attorney was at least smart enough to contact me before acting. I faxed a copy of the letter written by the insured, and he couldn't believe it. The case was closed there and then, but if I hadn't had that letter, which he couldn't deny because it was in his own handwriting and he couldn't say I had him sign a paper he didn't know what it meant. At that time, the state of Florida required that we write the coverage if the client wanted it—but they sure wouldn't back us up if we were sued for negligence. I guess I was just one step ahead of that client and his attorney and the state of Florida.

Free Country

People's right to choose their own morals, not the will of the party: The Spanish Inquisition ended in disaster because one of the ethnic groups was thrown out of the country. Our ethnicity is what has made us the most powerful nation on the planet.

Forty-five years ago, interracial marriage was illegal in fourteen states! In the 60s, young girls were dying because of the wire hangers used to abort fetuses. That's right, they met with some old woman in a back alley who performed an abortion with a wire hanger, and girls were dying in large numbers, bleeding to death, because the politicians thought it immoral to allow abortions. What kind of freedom do you think that implies? The technology was there to keep them safe, but the arrogance of those running this country to stand behind what was their morals or religious beliefs is astounding.

To this day, there are people wanting to overturn the amendment that allows licensed physicians and hospital facilities with sterile conditions to keep these girls safe as *they will seek abortions,* whether they are allowed to or not. On January 22, 1973, the US Supreme Court handed down its landmark decision, *Roe V. Wade,* recognizing the constitutional right to privacy and a woman's right to choose abortion. (http://www.plannedparenthoodaction. org/positions/roe-v-wade-643.htm)

We face those same issues today, as our leaders feel they have the right to impose their views of right and wrong upon the gay communities. These people didn't become gay because of some cult activity. Believe it or not, they were born that way, and our politicians are trying to interfere with the *Will of God* since they choose to put it that way. This is not the order of things, as one politician put it on "Meet The Press."

There are those who think we are children that must be controlled and take away our toys in the name of "gun control." The possibility of the existence of a weapon is a definite deterrent to a possible criminal, as the police certainly cannot defend what hasn't yet happened. Our forefathers placed in the Constitution the right to bear arms! Pretty smart, don't you think? The main reason was to allow the people to protect themselves from the very issue that is being brought out here. We have people whom we have placed in power to maintain the welfare of this nation and to protect and preserve our way of life, but that isn't what is happening here, is it?

How about a law that legislates *no impoverished children!* How do you explain to a six-year-old child that he or she must go to bed hungry? How do you explain we have no food or a place for them to lay their head to sleep? Everyone talks about the deficit! What exactly do you think that child—hungry, dirty from no place to clean up, tired from no place to sleep and feel secure, knows about the deficit? Our government is sending billions of dollars to countries all over the world to help other children, for whom we have no obligation. People that will eventually turn against us and kill our children. By the way, do you see where those people are benefiting from our money? It seems to me the people in charge are hoarding the money in vaults such as Saddam Hussein did in Iraq. He had vaults filled with US greenbacks. Why do these supposedly intelligent leaders borrow money from other countries so we can send it overseas while our children starve? What gives them the right to tell us they have to cut our entitlements, which by the way are entitlements **because** we paid for those benefits. What kind of morality is that?

In the 50s, I remember walking to the school bus every school day of the school year. We carried books that were so heavy we kept switching hands as they were getting sore and our arms strained. We walked through snow, sleet, rain, and hail! We walked even though the sun was so strong you could fry an egg on the street—but walk we did, as we had a responsibility to get to the bus on time so we could go to school. Why did we do this, you may ask? Because we were driven by the reality that if we didn't, we would catch hell from our parents.

Our parents supported the fact that we would go to school. Our parents made sure that we followed the rules. Our parents made sure we did our homework, and our parents worked with the teachers so that we would get an education.

Now, I don't want to sound like a speech writer, but that is exactly what is missing in our society: Parental participation! The teacher can only do so much to educate our young, but unless the child understands why they are learning what they are being taught, they will never understand and therefore actually learn. That is what is missing in our society! To memorize is not the same thing as learning, and reinforcement by the parents is tantamount to that process.

To regress back to the original part of this section, books need to be rewritten and updated. Books are heavy, as they are made of paper and cardboard. It takes trees to make paper and cardboard, and we are destroying and squandering our natural resources, not to mention the posture of our children, carrying those books in backpacks.

When you know that the entire world of knowledge is available through a tablet, why do we still do the same thing we did back in the early 1900s? Perhaps because it is the natural order of things, as one politician put it on "Meet the Press" one Sunday morning *while discussing the gay community.* What do you suppose is the meaning of the "natural order of things?" That which was correct but isn't anymore?

When do we wake up to the fact that this is a changing world, and if we do not change with that world, we are going to be left behind to eventually become a third-world country? Let us all make our first priority the same as in the Preamble to the Constitution, "secure the blessings of liberty to ourselves and *our posterity."*

For the sake of this country and what it stands for, let us all make the priority "our children!" We have the resources if only the top 1 percent would become a little less ambivalent and start thinking about the world instead of their own pocketbooks. We have the means to make this world a free world, free of dictatorship, tyranny, and persecution, where truly all are created equal. It all starts with education! It all starts with learning how to read, which is the biggest downfall of this nation. We have not stressed the art of reading properly, for if you can learn to read, you can learn anything. In order to learn to read, it takes teachers wanting to teach—but in order to get those kind of professionals, we must all realize that we have to pay them so they can devote their time and energy to teaching our children. Without that dedication, we will just destroy the greatest nation in the history of the world.

In this day and age, with technology moving as quickly as it has been and increasing exponentially, only a few will move forward, and the rest of us will eventually become slaves. Is that what you want? I don't think so! We must make a concerted effort to improve education and advance our children, or all will be lost! A teacher should have only one motive: bring those behind up to standard, and if they cannot do that, tenure should be eliminated as there are those that want to teach because it is a rewarding profession, not because it is a job. We have slipped all the way down to fourteenth in the world on education. We can and must change that by making sure we are once again number one. Now Mr. Politician, Mr. President, let's stop the excuses, roll up our sleeves, and make it happen. The people demand it! The future of this nation depends on it.

Allow me the honor of quoting a high school principal's speech as it is one of the most dynamic speeches I have ever had the privilege to encounter on the Internet.

Reproduced Speech by Dennis Prager of Colorado

To the students and faculty of our high school:

I am your new principal, and honored to be so. There is no greater calling than to teach young people.

I would like to apprise you of some important changes coming to our school. I am making these changes because I am convinced that most of the ideas that have dominated public education in America have worked against you, against your teachers, and against our country.

First, this school will no longer honor race or ethnicity. I could not care less if your racial makeup is black, brown, red, yellow, or white. I could not care less if your origins are African, Latin American, Asian, or European, or if your ancestors arrived here on the Mayflower or on slave ships. The only identity I care about, the only one this school will recognize, is your individual identity, your character, your scholarship, your humanity. And the only national identity this school will care about is American.

This is an American public school, and American public schools were created to make better Americans. If you wish to affirm an ethnic, racial, or religious identity through school, you will have to go elsewhere. We will end all ethnicity, race, and non-American nationality-based celebrations. They undermine the motto of America, one of its three central values: *e pluribus Unum*—from many, one." And this school will be guided by America's values. This includes all after-school clubs. I will not authorize clubs that divide students based on any identities. This includes race, language, religion, sexual orientation, or whatever else may become in vogue in society divided by political correctness.

Your clubs will be based on interests and passions, not blood, ethnic, racial, or other physically defined ties. Those clubs just cultivate narcissism—an unhealthy preoccupation with the self—while the purpose of education is to get you to think *beyond* yourself. So we will have clubs that transport you to the wonders and glories of art, music, astronomy, languages you do not already speak, carpentry, and more. If the only extracurricular activities you can imagine being interested in are those based on ethnic, racial, or sexual identity, that means that little outside of yourself really interests you.

Second, I am uninterested in whether English is your native language. My only interest in terms of language is that you leave this school speaking and writing English as fluently as possible. The English language has united America's citizens for over 200 years, and it will unite us at this school. It is one of the indispensable reasons this country of immigrants has always come to be one country. And if you leave this school without excellent English language skills, I would be remiss in my duty to ensure that you will be prepared to successfully compete in the American job market. We will learn other languages here—but if you want classes taught in your native language rather than in English, this is not your school.

Third, because I regard learning as a sacred endeavor, everything in this school will reflect learning's elevated status. This means, among other things, that you and your teachers will dress accordingly. Many people in our society dress more formally for Hollywood events than for church or school. These people have their priorities backward. Therefore, there will be a formal dress code at this school.

Fourth, no obscene language will be tolerated anywhere on this school's property—whether in class, in the hallways, or at athletic events. If you can't speak without using the f-word, you can't speak. By obscene language, I mean the words banned by the Federal Communications Commission, plus epithets such as "Nigger," even when used by one black student to address another black, or "bitch," even when addressed by a girl to a girlfriend. It is my intent that by the time you leave this school, you will be among the few your age to instinctively distinguish between the elevated and the degraded, the holy and obscene.

Fifth, we will end all self-esteem programs. In this school, self-esteem will be attained in only one way, the way people attained it until decided otherwise a generation ago—by earning it. One immediate consequence is that there will be one valedictorian, not eight.

Sixth and last, I am reorienting the school toward academics and away from politics and propaganda. No more time will be devoted to scaring you about smoking and caffeine or terrifying you about sexual harassment or global warming. No more semesters will be devoted to condom wearing and teaching you to regard sexual relations as only or primarily a health issue. There will be no more attempts to convince you that you are a victim because you are not white, or not male, or not heterosexual, or not Christian. We will have failed if any one of you graduates this school and does not consider him or herself inordinately lucky—to be alive and to be an American.

No expletives to follow as none needed. If any still hold trepidations as to the correctness herein expressed, perhaps it is lost in your values.

The Department of Homeland Security

Unfortunately the name *"Homeland"* brings back memories of another people. There are not too many people left today who can reference this name, but there are many who are aware of the name: " *Fatherland.*"

First there was the Patriot Act, which stripped the Bill of Rights, right out from under us, and now there is "The National Defense Authorization Act." No one ever thought this would be a war on the citizens of this country, and few would have discerned that it would ever set a stage for martial law.

One piece at a time. We are losing our precious freedom, and, like cows, we are just sitting by and letting it happen. We have people in Washington that are just thinking up ways to strip us of our constitutional right to the pursuit of happiness. Our currency has collapsed; our economy has been thrown into debt, which is unbearable; we are looking down the barrel of depression, and now we see military occupation being thrust upon our way of life.

Yea, go Republicans!

Yea, go Democrats!

Doesn't anyone have individual thinking today? You all seem so preoccupied with the party you are registered for that you forget to look at the person you are voting for. The Supreme Court says it is all right for corporations to donate to the candidates in any denomination they wish. Now we are being controlled by big money instead of that which has been shown by deed. How long does it take for the people to realize they are not part of the 1 percent? You might as well put a ring through your nose as you are being led to slaughter.

Indulge me and read something you ordinarily would not consider reading: the signing statement by President Obama of the defense bill. The complete signing will follow after I give to you my editorial impressions, should you decide to read it.

December 31, 2011

> The White House announced today from Hawaii that President Obama had signed into law a major defense policy bill but the President at the same time served notice to Congress that he would ignore certain provisions dealing with detainees in the war on terror.

Now if you are going to ignore certain provisions of a bill, shouldn't it stand to reason that you shouldn't sign the bill until it is correctly provided? It seems to me that one of the major problems with our system is that bills are signed for everyone else but Congress. Make it correct before you sign it, and do not sign it and expect to amend it later on! Examples such as in Section 1021: "My administration will interpret section 1021 in a manner that ensures that any detention it authorizes complies with the Constitution, the laws of war, and all other applicable law."

(Now there is a cute skirt if ever I heard one. The law is written but the present administration will interpret it one way while mentioning that the next administration may not follow suit. We cannot have laws that can be interpreted one way by one administration and another way by another administration. That, my friends, is exactly why we must stop these congressmen from changing authorities. The Constitution was set in stone, but they are only interested in changing it—and in so doing, destroying the very fiber of this great nation. I, for one, cannot comprehend why this bill was done in secrecy and why it took five hundred pages to create the destruction of our freedom.)

Section 1022: " While section 1022 is unnecessary and has the potential to create uncertainty, I have signed the bill because I believe that this section can be interpreted and applied in a manner that avoids undue harm to our current operations."

(Now that is a great reason to accept and sign the bill!)

"Absolute power corrupts absolutely." I put that in because I want you to think about that while you read the rest of the article. The following is as it was signed, FYI.

THE WHITE HOUSE
Office of the Press Secretary
FOR IMMEDIATE RELEASE
December 31, 2011

Statement by the President on H. R. 1540

Today I have signed into law H.R. 1540, the "National Defense Authorization Act for Fiscal Year 2012." I have signed the Act chiefly because it authorizes funding for the defense of the United States and its interests abroad, crucial services for service members and their families, and vital national security programs that must be renewed. In hundreds of separate sections totaling over five hundred pages, the Act also contains critical administration initiatives to control the spiraling health care costs of the Department of Defense, to develop counterterrorism initiatives abroad, to build the security capacity of key partners, to modernize the force, and to boost the efficiency and effectiveness of military operations worldwide.

The fact that I support this bill as a whole does not mean I agree with everything in it. In particular, I have signed this bill despite having serious reservations with certain provisions that regulate the detention, interrogation, and prosecution of suspected terrorists. Over the last several years, my administration has developed an effective sustainable framework for the detention, interrogation, and trial of suspected terrorists that allows us to maximize both our ability to collect intelligence and to incapacitate dangerous individuals in rapidly developing situations, and the results we have achieved are undeniable. Our success against Al-Qaida and its affiliates and adherents has derived in significant measure from providing our counterterrorism professionals with the clarity and flexibility they need to adapt to changing circumstances and to utilize whichever authorities best protect the American people and our accomplishments have respected the values that make our country an example for the world.

Against that record of success, some in Congress continue to insist upon restricting the options available to our counterterrorism professionals and interfering with the very operations that have kept us safe. My administration has consistently opposed such measures. Ultimately, I decided to sign this bill not only because of the critically important services it provides for our forces and their families and the national security programs it authorizes, but also because the Congress revised provisions that otherwise would have jeopardized the safety, security, and liberty of the American people. Moving forward, my administration will interpret and implement the provisions described below in a manner that best preserves the flexibility on which our safety depends and upholds the values on which this country was founded.

Section 1021 affirms the executive branch's authority to detain persons covered by the 2001 Authorization for Use of Military Force (AUMF) (Public Law 107-40;50 U.S.C. 1541 note). This section breaks no new ground and is unnecessary. The authority it describes was included in the 2001 AUMF, as recognized by the Supreme Court and confirmed through lower court decisions since then. Two critical limitations in section 1021 confirm that it solely codifies established authorities. First, under section 1021 (d), the bill does not "limit or expand the authority of the President or the scope of the Authorization for Use of Military Force." Second, under section 1021 (e), the bill may not be construed to affect any existing law or authorities relating to the detention of United States citizens, lawful resident aliens of the United States, or any other persons who are captured or arrested in the United States." My administration strongly supported the inclusion of these limitations in order to make clear beyond doubt that the legislation does nothing more than confirm authorities that the federal courts have recognized as lawful under the 2001 AUMF. Moreover, I want to clarify that my administration will not authorize the indefinite military detention without trial of American citizens. Indeed, I believe that doing so would break with our most important traditions and values as a nation. My administration will interpret section 1021 in a manner that ensures that any detention it authorizes complies with the Constitution, the laws of war, and all other applicable law.

Section 1022 seeks to require military custody for a narrow category of non-citizen detainees who are "captured in the course of hostilities authorized by the Authorization for Use of Military Force." This section is ill-conceived and will do nothing to improve the security of the United States. The executive branch already has the authority to detain in military custody those members of Al-Qaida who are captured in the course of hostilities authorized by the AUMF, and as commander in chief, I have directed the military to do so where appropriate. I reject any approach that would mandate military custody where law enforcement provides the best method of incapacitating a terrorist threat. While section 1022 is unnecessary and has the potential to create uncertainty, I have signed the bill because I believe that this section can be interpreted and applied in a manner that avoids undue harm to our current operations.

I have concluded that section 1022 provides the minimally acceptable amount of flexibility to protect national security. Specifically, I have signed this bill on the understanding that section 1022 provides the executive branch with broad authority to determine how best to implement it, and with the full and unencumbered ability to waive any military custody requirement, including the option of waiving appropriate categories of cases when doing so is in the national security interest of the United States. As my administration has made clear, the only responsible way to combat the threat Al-Qaida poses is to remain relentlessly practical, guided by the factual and legal complexities of each case and the relative strengths and weaknesses of each system. Otherwise, investigations could be compromised, our authorities to hold dangerous individuals could be jeopardized, and intelligence could be lost. I will not tolerate that result, and under no circumstances will my administration accept or adhere to a rigid across-the-board requirement for military detention. I will therefore interpret and implement section 1022 in the manner that best preserves the same flexible approach that has served us so well for the past three years and that protects the ability of law enforcement professionals to obtain the evidence and cooperation they need to protect the Nation.

My administration will design the implementation procedures authorized by section 1022 to provide the maximum measure of flexibility and clarity to our counterterrorism professionals permissible under law, and I will exercise all of my constitutional authorities as chief executive and commander in chief if those procedures fall short, including but not limited to seeking the revision or repeal of provisions should they prove to be unworkable.

(Why did you sign them in the first place?)

Sections 1023-1025 needlessly interfere with the executive branch's processes for reviewing the status of detainees. Going forward, consistent with congressional intent as detailed in the conference report, my administration will interpret section 1024 as granting the secretary of defense broad discretion to determine what detainee status determinations in Afghanistan are subject to the requirements of this section.

Sections 1026-1028 continue unwise funding restrictions that curtail options available to the executive branch. Section 1027 renews the bar against using appropriated funds for fiscal year 2012 to transfer Guantanamo detainees into the United States for any purpose. I continue to oppose this provision, which intrudes upon critical executive branch authority to determine when and where to prosecute Guantanamo detainees, based on the facts and the circumstances of each case and our national security interests. For decades, Republican and Democratic administrations have successfully prosecuted hundreds of terrorists in federal court. Those prosecutions are a legitimate, effective, and powerful tool in our efforts to protect the nation. Removing that tool from the executive branch does not serve our national security. Moreover, this intrusion would, under certain circumstances, violate constitutional separation of powers principles.

Section 1028 modifies but fundamentally maintains unwarranted restrictions on the executive branch's authority to transfer detainees to a foreign country. This hinders the executive's ability to carry out its military, national security, and foreign relations activities and like section 1027,would, under certain circumstances, violate constitutional separation of powers principles. The executive branch must have the flexibility to act swiftly in conducting negotiations with foreign countries regarding the circumstances of detainee transfers. In the event that the statutory restrictions in sections 1027 and 1028 operate in a manner that violates constitutional separation of powers principles, my administration will interpret them to avoid the constitutional conflict.

(Why authorize the bill in the first place if you can choose to not allow it to function?)

Section 1029 requires that the attorney general consult with the director of national intelligence and secretary of defense prior to filing criminal charges against or seeking an indictment of certain individuals. I sign this based on the understanding that apart from detainees held by the military outside of the United States under the 2001 Authorization for Use of Military Force, the provision applies only to those individuals who have been determined to be covered persons under section 1022 before the Justice Department files charges or seeks an indictment. Notwithstanding that limitation, this provision represents an intrusion into the functions and prerogatives of the Department of Justice and offends the longstanding legal tradition that decisions regarding criminal prosecutions should be vested with the attorney general, free from outside interference. Moreover, section 1029 could impede flexibility and hinder exigent operational judgments in a manner that damages our security. My administration will interpret and implement section 1029 in a manner that preserves the operational flexibility of our counterterrorism and law enforcement professionals, limits delays in the investigative process, ensures that critical executive branch functions are not inhibited, and preserves the integrity and independence of the Department of Justice.

Other provisions in this bill above could interfere with my constitutional foreign affairs powers. Section 1244 requires the president to submit a report to the Congress sixty days prior to sharing any US classified ballistic missile defense information with Russia, Section 1244 further specifies that this report include a detailed description of the classified information to be provided. While my administration intends to keep the Congress fully informed of the status of US efforts to cooperate with the Russian Federation on ballistic missile defense, my administration will also interpret and implement section 1244 in a manner that does not interfere with the president's constitutional authority to conduct foreign affairs and avoids the undue disclosure of sensitive diplomatic communications and national security secrets; and sections 1235, 1242, and 1245 would interfere with my constitutional authority to conduct foreign relations by directing the executive to take certain positions in negotiations or discussions with foreign governments. Like section 1244, should any application of these provisions conflict with my constitutional authorities, I will treat the provisions as non-binding.

My administration has worked tirelessly to reform or remove the provisions described above in order to facilitate the enactment of this vital legislation, but certain provisions remain concerning. My administration will aggressively seek to mitigate those concerns through the design of implementation procedures and other authorities available to me as chief executive and commander in chief, will oppose any attempt to extend or expand them in the future, and will seek the repeal of any provisions that undermine the policies and values that have guided my administration throughout my time in office.

Barack Obama

(Once again, why did you sign this bill? You already have decided you will not live by it so why did you sign it?)

According to the Bob Livingston Letter, this bill puts US citizens subject to military arrest under the pretense of being terrorists. Anyone can be arrested and detained indefinitely without trial. They can now make people disappear, never charge them, and hold them in prisons anywhere in the world. Due process of law is gone by legislation.

This bill has nothing to do with defense, as it is well known that the United States of America has the most powerful military ever devised, so it must be an attack on its citizens when they know with all that is going on, there is going to be some kind of backlash. What are these senators so frightened of? Is this a sign of things to come? Is this the beginning of the destruction of the rights guaranteed by Magna Carta, habeas corpus, or the right of personal liberty, forbidding government to arrest and hold any person without showing cause? This legislation will basically say in law for the first time that the *homeland* is part of the battlefield, as said by Sen. Lindsey Graham (R-S.C.) who supports this bill. This bill was drafted in secret by Senators Carl Levin (D-Mich.) and John McCain (R-Ariz.) before being passed in a closed-door committee meeting without any kind of hearing. Senator Mark Udall of Colorado said in a speech, "One section of these provisions, section 1031, would be interpreted as allowing the military to capture and indefinitely detain American citizens on US soil. Section 1031 essentially repeals the Posse Comitatus Act of 1878 authorizing the US military to perform law enforcement on American soil. Senator Udall set up a proposal to this legislation which would have stripped the detainees measures out of the NDAA but that proposal was defeated in the Senate. Small wonder!

Posse Comitatus Act

From Wikipedia (View original Wikipedia Article),last modified on 15 June 2012, at 13:21.

This article is about the Posse Comitatus Act in the United States. For other uses of posse comitatus, see Posse comitatus (disambiguation).

The Posse Comitatus Act is the United States federal law (18 U.S.C. § 1385, original at 20 Stat. 152) that was passed on June 18, 1878, after the end of Reconstruction. Its intent (in concert with the Insurrection Act of 1807) was to limit the powers of local governments and law enforcement agencies in using federal military personnel to enforce the laws of the land. Contrary to popular belief, the Act does not prohibit members of the Army from exercising state law enforcement, police or peace officer powers that maintain "law and order"; it simply requires that any authority to do so must exist with the United States Constitution or Act of Congress. In this way, most use of the Army and the Air Force at the direction of the president does not offend the statute, even though it may be problematic for other reasons (politically).

The statute only addresses the US Army and, since 1956, the US Air Force. It does not refer to, and thus does not restrict or apply to, the National Guard under state authority, acting in a law enforcement capacity within its home state or in an adjacent state if invited by that state's governor (in its federal capacity, the National Guard forms part of the Army or Air Force of the United States). The Navy and Marine Corps are prohibited by a Department of Defense directive (self-regulation), but not by the Act itself. Although it is a military force the US Coast Guard, which now operates under the Department of Homeland Security, is also not covered by the Posse Comitatus Act, primarily because the Coast Guard has both a maritime law enforcement mission and a federal regulatory agency mission.

A Political Pardon

Unfortunately, this country elects senators and congressmen who do not do what the people elected them to do. They usually have good intentions, but the only people running this country are the parties. We might do well to just vote in a party and save all the cost of the salaries and benefits, just like any other monotheistic nation of the world. I find it hard to comprehend that both parties are against deficit spending, yet we find them doing exactly that. They argue against high taxes and inflation, but we have both anyway. The president can only propose a budget while the House is responsible to either pass it or reject it. Why do you suppose they blame the current deficit on the president? The House has the checkbook! Whom do you suppose writes the tax code and sets fiscal policy?

There are no people representing the people, just parties. Let's get one thing perfectly clear! The Republican Party represents big money, which is why they told the average American we won't allow you the luxury of a continued tax break unless our rich boys, share in that luxury.

I am trying to understand the logic of the Republican Party when they talk about not raising the taxes on the _"job creators."_ If they were job creators, how come most of the jobs were sent overseas? Since NAFTA, we have lost about 50,000 factories, and that amounts to a lot of jobs.

The president wants to raise taxes on those that make in excess of $250,000 a year. Somehow, I cannot see the damage. If someone is earning over $250,000 per year, I think they can afford the small increase, especially when they are making over $250,000,000 per year. To hell with the middle and lower class! Yet, it is the middle class that votes those people in because, let's face it, the Democrats can't seem to agree on anything. If Washington really wanted this economy to grow, they are putting the money in the wrong hands. While Congress voted themselves an annual increase of $30,000, they also decided to freeze the increase of Social Security payments. How stupid could they possibly be? They took funds from the greatest spending group of people, because pockets to take it with them haven't been invented yet. You want to infuse funds into the economy? Therein lies the greatest vehicle you could have and while we are on the subject, you gave it to the banks and Wall Street people, the same people that sent the money overseas where it will never be seen again. Way to go, Congress!

The banks will not negotiate mortgages because if they foreclose, their losses are borne by the federal government. Where do those funds come from? The very same people that are being foreclosed upon. How about the federal government cutting its losses by renegotiating with the homeowner for a reasonable compromise. Did you ever stop to think that with so much unemployment and decrease of spending by those on Social Security we have the economic meltdown as it is today? Did you ever stop to think, since so many are unemployed we have the only people, supporting the federal budget, unable to support the federal budget? Now tell me the super rich shouldn't get a tax hike when they, the "job creators" have created this problem in the first place. Oh yes! A real intelligent group running this country!

When you consider that there are 435 congressmen, a hundred senators, one president and nine Supreme Court justices fulfilling the needs of 310 million people, it makes me shudder that they are doing such a poor job of it. Did you ever think about the fact that when a member of Congress gets voted out, he continues to get the same salary and benefits? Why is that? Why do you suppose they fight so hard just to keep the benefits they get anyway? Do you suppose while in office there is some underlying reason? Exactly what is the function of the lobbyists? Since they have no authority, how do you suppose they can be effective? To my knowledge it is illegal to accept bribes, so what are the lobbyists doing? Surely if they are offering something that is not within the parameters of the congressman's purview and that incentive is taken, isn't that illegal? I for one feel it is the congressman's obligation to vote what he feels is in the best interest of the country even if offered $1 million to vote in favor of the lobbyist. Now, I am not saying our congressional publically elected officials would do such a thing, but please ask yourself, why are there lobbyists? Exactly what is their function?

In 1913, congress appointed the Federal Reserve Board and delegated upon them the duty to provide a sound currency to a federally chartered but private central bank. I see we are getting our money's worth! Just like guilty people, all claim the fault is on the other guy and refuse to take responsibility for their actions.

Allow me to define a stimulus package:

In Littletown, USA, a salesman decides to check into a hotel. Let me see the rooms first and to show my sincerity, I will put this hundred-dollar bill down on your counter first. Of course, the innkeeper agrees and has his assistant show the salesman around. Just that quickly, the innkeeper takes the hundred-dollar bill across the street to pay the butcher that which is overdue. The butcher, now having been paid off from the hotel owner, takes the hundred-dollar bill and pays off the funds he owes the farmer. Now business has been so bad in the town that the local prostitute has had to perform her job on credit and the farmer now owes $100 to her, which he immediately brings to her to eliminate that which he owes. The prostitute runs down the street to pay off the hotel bill she owes. Now, the salesman comes down the stairs advising he is not satisfied and will move on to the next town as he picks up his hundred-dollar bill and leaves. No one has produced any products, no one has earned anything—but now all debts have been satisfied. And that, my friend, is how a stimulus package works.

What has been done to bring the manufacturing jobs back to what was at one point the greatest industrial nation in the world? Comes now again the *pendulum*. It swings only so far in one direction and then reverses itself. When there are no people that can afford to buy products, the demand becomes moot, and this country, which was the largest purchasing society of the world, will no longer be a purchasing power because, no jobs, no money, no need for products. Way to go, Congress! Even the overseas industries are slowing down because they cannot sell their products. The economy of the world is faltering, but our political system of over-stuffed shirts will not do anything about it! All the money in the world has been put to sleep, hoarded by the 1 percent that cannot see the forest, for the trees block their view.

The law of the land, the Constitution of the United States, has written it in stone that the House of Representatives has full authority and responsibility of originating and approving appropriations and taxes.

Section 7 of the Constitution is as follows:

All Bills for raising revenue shall originate in the House of Representatives; but the Senate may propose or concur with Amendments as on other Bills.

Every Bill which shall have passed the House of Representatives and the Senate, shall, before it becomes a law be presented to the President of the United States: If he approves he shall sign it, but if not he shall return it with his objections to that House in which it shall have originated, who shall enter the objections at large on their journal and proceed to reconsider it. If after such reconsideration two-thirds of that House shall agree to pass the bill, it shall be sent, together with the objections, to the other House, by which it shall likewise be reconsidered, and if approved by two-thirds of that House, it shall become a Law. But in all such cases the votes of both Houses shall be determined by yeas and nays, and the names of the persons voting for and against the bill shall be entered on the Journal of each House respectively. If any bill shall not be returned by the President within ten days (Sundays excepted) after it shall have been presented to him, the same shall be a Law in like manner as if he had signed it, unless the Congress by their adjournment prevents its return, in which case it shall not be a Law.

Clear as Mud!

Every Order, Resolution, or Vote to which the Concurrence of the Senate and House of Representatives may be necessary (except on a question of Adjournment) shall be presented to the President of the United States; and before the Same shall take Effect, shall be approved by him, or being disapproved by him, shall be re passed by two-thirds of the Senate and House of Representatives, according to the rules and Limitations prescribed in the Case of a Bill.

Section 8

The Congress shall have Power To lay and collect Taxes, Duties, Imposts and Excises to pay the Debts and provide for the common Defense and General Welfare of the United States but all duties, Imposts and Excises shall be uniform throughout the United States:

To borrow Money on the credit of the United States:

To regulate Commerce with foreign Nations and among the several States, and with the Indian Tribes:

To establish a uniform rule of Naturalization and uniform Laws on the subject of Bankruptcies throughout the United States:

To coin Money, regulate the Value thereof and of foreign Coin and fix the Standard of Weights and Measures:

To provide for the Punishment of counterfeiting the Securities and current Coin of the United States:

To establish Post Offices and Post Roads:

To promote the Progress of Science and useful Arts, by securing for limited Times to Authors and Inventors the exclusive Right to their respective Writings and Discoveries:

To constitute Tribunals inferior to the Supreme Court:

To define and punish Piracies and Felonies committed on the high Seas and Offences against the Law of Nations:

To declare War, grant Letters of Marque and Reprisal and make Rules concerning Captures on Land and Water:

To raise and support Armies but no appropriation of Money to that Use shall be for a longer Term than two years:

To provide and maintain a Navy:

To make rules for the Government and Regulation of the land and naval forces:

To provide for calling forth the Militia to execute the Laws of the Union, suppress Insurrections and repel Invasions:

To provide for organizing, arming, and disciplining, the Militia, and for governing such part of them as may be employed in the Service of the United States, reserving to the States respectively, the Appointment of the Officers, and the Authority of training the Militia according to the discipline prescribed by Congress:

To exercise exclusive Legislation in all Cases whatsoever, over such District (not exceeding ten Miles square) as may by Cession of particular States, and the Acceptance of Congress, become the Seat of the Government of the United States, and to exercise like Authority over all Places purchased by the Consent of the Legislature of the State in which the Same shall be, for the erection of Forts, Magazines, Arsenals, dock—Yards and other needful buildings and

To make all Laws which shall be necessary and proper for carrying into Execution the foregoing Powers and all other Powers vested by this Constitution in the Government of the United States, or in any Department or Officer thereof.

The arrogance of the speaker of the house to place blame on the president of the United States for the budget they (the House of Representatives) can establish even over the presidential veto, in my opinion, is astonishing to say the least on a level that is staggering at this point in time. It stands to reason that whatever is wrong with the economy of this nation is because they want it to be wrong. Five hundred and forty-five people are responsible to 310 million people for the agony they are enduring today, and it is all incompetence and greed along with a lust for power that brings this all about. If they don't like the tax code, fix it! If we are in the red budget-wise, fix it.

Congress is the only organization that sets up rules to fit their circumstances without regard to the people. They are the only people that can campaign to get something set and then vote it down. Why are they on a different retirement system and health care system than the rest of us? If they were in the same system as we, they would fix it. It is because they want it that way! It is as it is. The fact that we are still at war with other nations is because they want us to be at war with other nations. You know there were never any weapons of mass destruction in Iraq and yet our intelligent Congress, with zero evidence accepted, the sales job from G. W. Bush and Dick Cheney and allowed for us to go to war. I wonder how much money for the defense budget actually goes to the companies we contract!

You, the American people are given a choice of two individuals running for the office of president of The United States of which you must choose one. The party is the deciding factor. You carry on like a bunch of students at a football game being emotionally excited by a bunch of cheerleaders. Which party are you going to vote for? You are angry because a group of radical Muslims have carried out such horrific plans, but you yourselves show nothing but radical behavior. Are you going to stand for the country being at a total standstill to create the illusion that the other party is at fault for the problems we suffer? Isn't it obvious enough that you are being influenced?

To hell with the party! Vote your conscience and vote for the person. Should it matter what party affiliation they are? We hire these representatives to represent the people and bring about a cohesive relationship to get done that which needs to be done. I don't remember hiring the party or its philosophies. I cannot believe we voted for a bunch of children that just want to bicker and complain rather than do their job.

We need some new rules in this game. Let's get one thing perfectly clear, to coin a phrase, when running for office, seeking the approval of the American people by their votes, *tell us not what is bad about the other person running against you, tell us what is right with your accomplishments, what you stand for and what you plan on doing in our behalf!*

This idea of negative advertising is seen all over the world and we appear as the children we are. We must show leadership in that we are the most powerful nation on the planet. How secure do you think the people of the world are when you show immaturity that at any moment we might make an irresponsible decision and blow up the world. We need a third party with enough power to put up a candidate as well as candidates for the House and Senate. The way I see it, there will be a billion dollars chasing a million dollars.

There should be a budget for each candidate, and not the ridiculous one approved by the Supreme Court. I am sorry, but you cannot draw blood from a corporation. Corporations are non-entity, non-corporeal organizations and should not have the right to donate unlimited values, thereby influencing the turnout of an election. They haven't the right to vote, so why do they have the right to influence policies that affect the lives of the people? This is a country that claims to be *"Of the people, by the people, and for the people,"* I haven't seen anything there that mentions corporations.

At this very moment, deals are being made for donations, and those deals aren't in anyway helpful for the economy or the people. I hope you understand what I am implying here! You have been placed in a position whereby you cannot even help the candidate of your choice because you cannot afford to support that candidate. Do you think perhaps this is by design? Most of us donate, in our tax returns, $2 per person. Assuming, due to economic times, there are only 50 million people working, that equates to $100 million per tax year; over four years, that amounts to $400 million, which should be sufficient for anyone to run for the office of the president of The United States of America, but that isn't a drop in the bucket when you consider the millions of dollars being donated by corporations, *right*? Power to the corporations, not the people.

The people have their chance now come November. You can either accept all those lies told to you or you can break the backs of the corporations conspiring against you. You decide! Do not allow them to con you into believing there exists some mystical force such as the economy or inflation or politics that dissuades them from correctly doing that which they are sworn to do. Wake up America, and don't be fooled by fear. The only thing we have to fear is fear itself, and I believe that was said before.

These corporations depend on a symbiotic existence and all realize that there is something known as an *import tax* that was devised by our forefathers to protect our workers. Why Congress has not used it is beyond belief on a level that is staggering at this point in time. When we export to other countries, we are charged an import tax which makes sense, but when we import, we are charging a ridiculous percentage somewhere around 4 percent as opposed to 20 percent or 40 percent. This must stop.

Congress refuses to act to the needs of the people, so perhaps the people should begin to act in their own behalf. When you go to the store to purchase anything, do you look first to see where that item is made? I have taken notice and found that even Wolverine shoes aren't made here in this country. I have, however, noticed that many of the tools sold in Sears are made in the USA. I have looked for a TV that is made here, and I cannot find one. I would have been willing to pay a little more for one made in the USA, but none were available or at least, not that I could find. Start taking notice. Hershey candy tells me on the package that this candy was made in Mexico. Now, there was a factory in Hershey, Pennsylvania that has been handed down from generation to generation, but now manufactured in Mexico. I personally will not buy their products anymore, as I am angry that people in this country have lost their jobs because those jobs were exported.

You can make a difference. Make those items you have last longer. Do not purchase anything made elsewhere, like China, unless it is absolutely imperative that you do so. I feel sure the companies that have exported your jobs will get the picture. Make a conscious effort to support our own people first! Congress seems to be economically motivated. Let's see if we can get them motivated for the benefit of the people and not the corporations.

Allow me to list as many taxes imposed on the people of this country as I can muster up, and you be the judge:

Federal Income Tax, State Income Tax, Federal Sales Tax, State Sales Tax, Gasoline Tax, Cigarette Tax, Alcohol Tax, Federal Utility Tax, State Utility Tax, Telephone Tax, Federal, State, and Local including Excise, Telephone Usage Tax, including Minimum Usage, Personal Property Tax (Advalorem Tax), Corporate & Commercial Property Tax, Local and State License Fees, Automobile License Fees, Driver License Fees, Boat License Fees, Motorcycle License Fees, CDL License Fees, Commercial Vehicles License Fees, Taxes on Interstate Trucking, Rental Tax, Inheritance Tax, Social Security Tax, Unemployment Tax, SUTA and FUTA, Professional License Fees, 411 Charge (now there is a good one, as you get charged for each phone but you can only use one to make the call), Marriage License Tax, Luxury Taxes, IRS penalties (which is a tax on top of a tax), Excise Taxes, Pet License Taxes, Fishing License Tax, Hunting License Fees, Commercial Fishing License Fees, Fuel Permit Tax, Alcohol, Beer & Wine License, Gross Receipts Tax, Inventory Tax, Real Estate Tax, Service Charge Tax, Road Usage (Tolls), School Tax, Well Permit Tax, Excess Surplus Lines Tax (out of state usage tax), Import Taxes however small they be, Cable TV

Tax, ISP Tax, Occupational license fees, Elevator license fees

I am probably remiss by leaving many out because I cannot think of any more. I do not believe that, in the year 1900, any of these taxes existed, yet we thrived and had the most prosperous nation on the planet. There was no national debt, and the middle class was huge enough to probably be the largest in the world.

Warren Buffett recently said in an interview on CNBC, "Just pass a law that states, anytime there is a deficit of more than 3 percent GDP, all sitting members of Congress are *ineligible for re-election*." He should have added that they would lose their benefits also.

Why are Congress people allowed to do what everyone else in the nation is held legally liable for? Manipulation of the stock market?

Why haven't any bankers, with the exception of a sperm bank owner in L.A., been prosecuted and if found guilty, sent directly to jail without passing *go*? *If,* now that is a joke!

Why hasn't a former president been impeached for sending this nation to war with a nation that has not attacked us which is a breach to the Constitution of the United States of America?

Why were there two organizations created for the mortgage market by that president, whereby the president of each earned between eight and nine times the salary of the president of The United States?

Why, if they were found to be guilty of federal law violation as well as violation of the public trust, haven't they been thrown into prison? Bernie sure was!

Wall Street banks helped to cause the worst economic crisis since the Great Depression. Why haven't we held them accountable? Millions of homes, retirement saving programs, and jobs were lost and the largest of those banks gave their executives a whopping $145 billion in bonuses. Don't you find that appalling? The result was bad enough, but to reward them on top, absolutely absurd! To think we went and gave them the funds to pay those bonuses!

Troubled Asset Relief Program

For those of you that are unaware, the acronym is *TARP*, and it was signed into law by G. W. Bush on October 3, 2008. Somehow, it appears to me that the blame for what came about after fell on Barack Obama! You know, the president who didn't sign it into law!

The function of TARP was to purchase assets and equity from financial institutions. The concept was to strengthen those institutions financially to address the sub-prime mortgage crisis. Originally, the program authorized $700 *billion*. A point of interest: the sub-prime mortgage problem didn't come about because money was made more accessible to people who were unable to pay but rather because the amount of money earned in commissions for the brokers was higher and many of the people with sufficient funds for a down payment were placed in those mortgages and never told exactly how the variableness of that mortgage was going to be implemented. For example, it never should have been allowed for a mortgage to start at $1,200 per month, principal and interest, which is probably affordable on a house valued at about $300,000 but mortgaged at less than $200,000. But when it jumps up to $1,900 per month—on a house now devalued to about $100,000. Any person with any kind of intelligence would tell the bank to go you-know-where, and that is what brought about the crisis. In simple terms, it was *greed on the part of the bank* that brought this crisis to light, so please stop blaming the people and saying they bought a house they couldn't afford! That is nothing but a bald-faced lie.

Now, taking into consideration the banks were backed by the federal government, TARP left them in a position whereby negotiations with the people would bring about a loss, which should have been negotiated out so both the lender and the borrower took a loss. The bank, who is now the seller, sells this home for around $65,000 and turns the loss over to, you guessed it, the federal government and says, now look, I took a loss, so pay me. Now, where do you suppose those funds came from? You are smart! The same people that were just foreclosed on. But they choose to blame it on the homeowner that probably would have negotiated with the bank for a lower mortgage. I understand the amount payable by the Fed is 80 percent of the original price of the home. Too good to pass up, right?

If you really want to know about TARP, I suggest you bring up Wikipedia on your computer and type in TARP. You will be amazed at what has transpired right under your nose—and you voted in those people.

Many years ago, if you were overdrawn in your checking account, depending on your relationship with your banker, you may have gotten a phone call asking you to tend to that issue immediately. Sometimes, if your relationship wasn't that good, the check would bounce, and you had to deal with the recipient, personally. Today the bank seeks other checks that would have gone through and cashes the larger one first, causing instead of just one bounce, perhaps three—at $35 to $40 in fees per check—thus causing other checks to bounce, even though you corrected the situation immediately. This creates a chain reaction which grows to epidemic proportions. Now, I want you to please keep in mind that in the preface of this book, I mentioned this was all opinions expressed by an ordinary person's perception of how he sees these issues. I wonder how many of you reading this chapter have the same perceptions and wonder why rules haven't been placed to prevent this type of activity instead of allowing it to just fester like a pre-cancer cell on the move. Do you feel our government is doing the best job with the interest of the people in mind? Do you think there are any politicians today that could stand up to George Washington, Thomas Jefferson, John Hancock, Abraham Lincoln, Franklin D. Roosevelt, or even Harry S. Truman?

I rest my case!

Trickle Trickle

"Boom, trickle trickle, stomp stomp, tell me about the words of love." Words from a song, I believe from the 60s. The reality is, let's discuss the issue of *trickle-down economics*.

Theoretically, it is a sound issue, but now, when you throw in the human greed factor, it no longer is a viable concept. Supposedly, if you give funds to the wealthy, they will take care of the not-so-wealthy. This is truly a Republican concept, which is why <u>the upper four hundred people on the economic table have more wealth than the lower 150 million combined.</u> Wow! Now that seems quite profound—and they say all men are created equal!

Let's see now, what would I do if I were a very wealthy man? First, I would become paranoid that everyone was trying to take my wealth. I would have to make some kind of plan to hide that money so that I could keep it out of the hands of those greedy lawyers. Strange, I would need a lawyer to help me to do just that. Poetic Justice! In an effort to now breach the anti-money-laundering laws, I will have to declare the money and pay zero dollars in taxes, and then I can ship it to some foreign bank where I become judgment-proof. There are a few countries that do nothing else but banking, and they have strict laws about divulging personal information and will not yield to the federal government of the United States. Through various trusts, I can hide the other assets and *poof! I am judgment-proof.* I have eliminated the lollypop those greedy lawyers want, and therefore none of them will want to sue me because they might never get paid. *Hide the lollypop game!*

Making obscene profits from the money loaned to me by the federal government, which isn't mine and I do have to pay it back at a ridiculously low rate of interest, making that money judgment-proof (it isn't an asset of mine because it is borrowed from the United States Treasury). I am now in business with your money and making obscene profits with absolutely no risk whatsoever. I have created very few jobs—and paid very low salaries to those employees. *How to create slavery 101.* Wake up people, 95 percent of the wealth of this nation is in the hands of 5 percent of the population!

Obamacare

Without getting too technical, I am going to try to impart to you the actual need for a socialized medicine system for the United States of America. Please understand, I am a licensed insurance agent, licensed in every capacity of insurance, which is to say that I have a little knowledge of how insurance works. But, according to the medical people, I probably would be told I have no idea what I am talking about. It seems to them this is the worst thing to happen since HMOs. Perhaps even worse than income taxes!

Have you ever wondered what the cost of drugs actually is? I mean the actual cost of the ingredients? I am going to try to display some of the most popular drugs and their cost. I have gotten this list from an e-mail that came from Sharon L. Davis, budget analyst, US Department of Commerce; Mary Palmer, budget analyst, Bureau of Economic Analysis Office of Budget & Finance and Diane Foster, contracting officer, and this information is from 06/02/2005. The information here was given with a request that we pass it along to everyone.

Celebrex, 100 mg.
Consumer price (100 tablets):	$130.27
Cost of general active ingredients:	$0.60
Percent markup:	21,712%

Claritin, 10 mg.
Consumer price (100 tablets):	$215.17

Cost of general active ingredients:	$0.71
Percent markup:	30,306%

Keflex, 250 mg.

Consumer price (100 tablets):	$157.39
Cost of general active ingredients:	$1.88
Percent markup:	8,372%

Lipitor, 20 mg.

Consumer price (100 tablets):	$272.37
Cost of general active ingredients:	$5.80
Percent markup:	4,696%

The list goes on and on, and the percentage of markup is just as astounding for each drug. Couple this with the refusal to cure any complications, just treat them, and you can see why the cost of medicine is in the range of 17 percent of our GDP.

What is GDP? I am going to quote Wikipedia on this one: "Gross Domestic Product (GDP) is the value of all goods and services produced in the United States. The GDP figure is released quarterly.

"How it's used: GDP is used to measure economic output. The growth rate in GDP is closely evaluated by the Federal Reserve to determine whether the economy is growing too slowly or too quickly. Recessions are often defined as two consecutive quarters of contraction in GDP."

Now let's get to the other end of the spectrum and discuss the doctors. I recently went to the dermatologist, where I spent about one-half hour, of which I was in the exam room only about ten minutes. By the way, I must compliment that doctor, as most keep you in the waiting room about forty-five minutes alone, before seeing you. He was so efficient he was able to slice off a wart about one-quarter inch in diameter, remove some small growth from my ear, remove some moles from my back, and destroy some benign or premalignant lesions. Now let's get to the cost factors.

Procedure:	Cost	Eligible	Paid
Office/ outpatient visit:	$ 135.00	$112.51	$ 97.93
Biopsy of external ear:	$ 275.00	$ 55.06	$ 55.30
Biopsy of skin lesion	$ 190.00	$ 55.60	$ 55.84
Biopsy skin subq/mucous	$ 570.00	$ 105.56	$ 106.11
Tissue exam by pathologist	$ 1,125.00	$ 552.95	$ 555.31
Destroy flat wart up to 14 lesions	$ 175.00	$ 117.94	$ 118.44
Destroy benign/ premalignant lesion	$ 150.00	$ 43.28	$0000.00

Totals	
Billed	$2,620.00
Eligible	$1,043.00
Ineligible	$43.28

Interest	$4.21
Amount paid	$ 988.93

Now that to me says they were paid between 37 percent and 38 percent of what they charged. I wonder what the lab was actually paid.

Now let's assume I was a person without insurance. I am sure I would have been billed the full amount, and maybe I would have been able to negotiate the bill down to about $2,000, assuming I was an excellent negotiator. This is exactly why we need a socialized medicine system—the wise guys are running away with themselves. Imagine, I was only one person there, and there were several others waiting when I left. My wife was also there, but I am not going to tell you her episode. Please keep in mind that the entire episode only ran for about ten minutes. That is exactly why we need a medical insurance program that watches over the doctors or they would be soaking us to maybe 40 percent GDP if left alone.

President after president had promised a socialized medicine system and never delivered. Obama realized the GDP needed some serious attention. He also realized there were many inequities created, as the doctors had to bring patients to court to collect. Very often the final result was not that the medical fees were paid but legal fees had to be paid. Many indigent people were going to the emergency room for minor medical problems because they couldn't pay the deductible in share of cost, while Medicaid would pay the full bill if it were over the amount of the share of cost deductible. Can you imagine a hangnail costing around $2,000? If it were taken care of in the doctor's office, it probably would have been billed out at maybe $100, plus the cost of antibiotic. The patient would have to have paid the entire amount, assuming the doctor would see the patient at all. We, the United States of America, are the only industrialized nation on the planet without such a system. Why do you suppose that is? Who do you suppose was the organization lobbying to keep socialized medicine out of this country? Seems strange to me how one man had enough guts to take on the lobbyists and take the interest of the people to heart. One individual told me the only interest that will really profit here are the insurance companies. Have you taken a look around? Do you not see the insurance companies have abandoned the health insurance field because it was a loser? What do you have today? Third-party administrators—because they do not have the same constraints as the insurance companies. We cannot allow this runaway inflationary spiral to continue, or it will cost your firstborn just for a flu! There must be controls, and even after that, the doctors will still make more than they are entitled to, but they will complain for a while and not consider the Hippocratic Oath they took as they have forsaken the people with preexisting conditions. Hey, if you haven't any insurance or are poor, you have the right to just die. Sorry, but I have got to make my profit!

It is about time we started taking care of our own people, who have been neglected far too long. It is about time we began taking care of our veterans, our poor, our tired, and our sick. Our children and their abandoned mothers. Our homeless—and thank heaven we do not have to mention our elderly, as they already have a system in place, one which heard the same cries as to how it was going to bankrupt our country. Social Security also heard that cry, and in case you do not remember, we heard the same cry when the computer age came about. Fear is how things are held back, and it is about time we woke up and began to advance to a new world in which all people have an opportunity to live a good and decent life.

The Sports Tattler

Isn't professional sports a wonderful pastime for all? Most American people take a great interest in sports, and many choose different sports to be their favorite. Make no mistake about it, there is a tremendous amount of money connected with professional sports. For example, in 2009, the revenue for the NFL exceeded $7.8 billion. The revenue for the MLB exceeded $6.8 billion and the NBA exceeded $4 billion. Many of the players were paid salaries in the millions of dollars.

Why go to college and get good grades? You most likely wouldn't make that kind of money! So just be good at a sport. Of course, you could always go back to school when you are a millionaire and retired from the sport. Don't waste those youthful years, as there is too much money to be made while you are young. It doesn't matter if you are past your prime; if you have a special name, you can bring in more revenue. Don't give someone else a chance to get in because there is still too much money to just walk away—remember Brett Favre? Oh! And you can go ahead and be cruel to animals with an illegal betting game; you can even go to prison, and when you get out, you can be relicensed and contracted with a tremendous salary, just like Michael Vick.

The thing that gripes me the most is that there is a vast supply of people, volunteers, that work very hard supporting these sports. Isn't that nice? The NFL in 2011 took in $9 billion. The players took home millions of dollars playing the game, and those volunteers who busted their asses making the event run smoothly took home nothing. Somehow, something seems to elude me. Don't you think that should be illegal? I wonder if I could get someone to volunteer to mow my lawn or wash my car or paint my house?

I can understand volunteers in the universities' sports programs, as the funds coming out of their activities help support the school system. The funds also supply scholarships for many of the students, especially some of the great athletes that would never get a chance to go to a university, graduate with a substantial degree, and go play games to earn millions of dollars per year.

In the beginning, sports were played on a voluntary basis and mainly for the fun of it. The players weren't paid, but they still played with all the zest and vigor that anyone could possibly tie to pride. Then one day someone got the idea that there could be a lot of money made here, and professional sports became the big business it is today. No one could possibly feel as though this is a bad thing, but when so much money is being made, why on God's little green apple aren't the volunteers paid? Look at all the wasted employment when jobs are so scarce.

The Peace-Loving Country Known as the United States of America

We are probably the most peace-loving nation in the history of the world, right?

Excreta Taurus!

Excreta taurus, better known as bullshit, spread by our leaders as they set us up for the next killer war. I'll bet there isn't a handful of people out there who are capable of reciting most of the wars we have been involved in. However, thanks to a publisher of a little-known newspaper known as the *Pineapple Post,* I can list most of the wars. At this juncture, I wish to give my thanks to Michael Purcell for his article, which I am going now to transcribe here for you.

This article was placed in the *Pineapple Post* in the May 15, 2012 edition.

Memorial Day is around the corner, which kicks off the summer season for many. For others, it is a somber reminder of war times, lost comrades, lifelong injuries, post-traumatic stress disorders, and the process of calling the memories left over from horrific times.

The American Flag stands for many symbolic sacrifices. On Memorial Day weekend, everyone, from all parts of the globe (who reside within the boundaries of the United States), should pay homage to those who fought for the freedoms we all take for granted. Many of us have never lived abroad or in places of horrible living conditions. Many have never gone hungry or worried if they were going to have a home in the morning to wake up to. When the oppression of governments has squeezed the freedoms out of its citizens, where do they dream of coming? The country that has stood for freedom, choices, and the ability to prosper has been and continues to be the United States of America.

Memorial Day was originally named "Decoration Day" by Union soldiers after the Civil War (which claimed the lives of over 600,000 soldiers) had ended in 1868. After noticing how the Confederate soldiers had honored its fallen soldiers, Union General John Logan adopted the concept and, as head of a veterans group called the "Grand Army of the Republic," used his influence to create Decoration Day and to encourage all Americans to recognize the need to observe those who had fallen in war. On May 30, 1868, the graves of both Confederate and Union soldiers were decorated with flowers and ribbons, but Decoration Day was not celebrated by the South until after WW I. In 1967, Congress changed the holiday from Decoration Day to Memorial Day and in 1971, made it an official holiday to honor fallen soldiers of all wars.

What started as an observance of deceased soldiers of a war of a divided country has since become a moment in time to show respect for soldiers fighting in a "now unified" country.

The following is a list of most of the wars the United States has been involved in:

American Revolutionary War
Northwest Indian War
Quasi-War, aka Franco-American War
First Barbary War
Tecumseh's War
War of 1812
Second Barbary War
First Seminole War
Arikara War
Winnebago War
Black Hawk War
Second Seminole War
Mexican American War
Navajo Wars
Cayuse War
Apache Wars
Yakima War
Rogue Rivers War
Puget Sound War
Third Seminole War
Second Opium War
Reform War
Paiute War
American Civil War
Dakota War of 1862
Colorado War
Snake War

Red Cloud's War
Comanche War
Modoc War
Red River War
Black Hills War
Nez Perce War
Bannock War
Cheyenne War
White River War
Sheepeater Indian War
Second Anglo-Egyptian War (the Egyptian expedition)
Columbian Civil War (the Burning of Colón)
First Samoan Civil War
Ghost Dance War
Chilean Civil War
Second Samoan Civil War
Spanish-American War
Philippines—American War
Banana Wars (including the US occupation of
    Nicaragua, Haiti, and the Dominican Republic)
The Boxer Rebellion
Mexican Revolution
World War I
Russian Civil War
World War II
Cold War (not a real war)
First Indochina War
Korean War
Vietnam War
Laotian Civil War
Cambodian Civil War
Lebanese Civil War
Iran—Iraq War

Gulf War
Somali Civil War
Bosnian War
Kosovo War
War on Terror
War in Afghanistan
Iraq War
Second Liberian Civil War
Libyan Civil War

Now, does that sound like a peace-loving nation?

European Life Died in Auschwitz

The following is an article I received in my e-mail. I felt it was such a strong message that I felt compelled to place it in this book. It is an article that appeared in a Spanish newspaper on January 15, 2008 and was written by Sebastian Vilar Rodrigez:

> I walked down the street in Barcelona, and suddenly discovered a terrible truth: Europe died in Auschwitz . . . We killed six million Jews and replaced them with twenty million Muslims. In Auschwitz, we burned a culture, thought, creativity, talent. We destroyed the chosen people, truly chosen, because they produced great and wonderful people who changed the world.

> The contribution of this people is felt in all areas of life: science, art, international trade, and above all, as the conscience of the world. These are the people we burned.

> Under the pretense of tolerance, and because we wanted to prove to ourselves that we were cured of the disease of racism, we opened our gates to twenty million Muslims, who brought us stupidity and ignorance, religious extremism and lack of tolerance, crime and poverty, due to an unwillingness to work and support their families with pride.

They have blown up our trains and turned our beautiful Spanish cities into the third world, drowning in filth and crime.

Shut up in the apartments they receive free from the government, they plan the murder and destruction of their naive hosts.

Thus, in our misery, we have exchanged culture for fanatical hatred, creative skill for destructive skill, intelligence for backwardness and superstition.

We have exchanged the pursuit of peace of the Jews of Europe and their talent for a better future for their children, their determined clinging to life because life is holy, for those who pursue death, for people consumed by the desire for death for themselves and others, for our children and theirs.

What a terrible mistake was made by miserable Europe.

A lot of Americans have become so insulated from reality that they imagine America can suffer defeat without any inconvenience to themselves.

Recently, the U.K. debated whether to remove the Holocaust from its school curriculum because it "offends" the Muslim population, which claims it never occurred. It is not removed as yet. However, this is a frightening portent of the fear that is gripping the world and how easily each country is giving in to it.

It is now more than sixty years after the Second World War in Europe ended. This e-mail is being sent as a memorial chain, in memory of the six million Jews, twenty million Russians, ten million Christians, and 1,900 Catholic priests who were "murdered, raped, burned, starved, beaten, experimented on and humiliated." Now, more than ever, with Iran, among others, claiming the Holocaust to be "a myth," it is imperative to make sure the world never forgets.

This e-mail is intended to reach four hundred million people. Be a link in the memorial chain and help distribute this around the world.

How many years will it be before the attack on the World Trade Center, *"never happened"* because it offends some Muslim in the United States?

Do not just delete this message; it will take only a minute to pass this along.

Wake up America before it's too late!

I would like to add at this juncture that General Eisenhower told the press to take as many pictures as possible of the concentration camps as one day, some would try to deny the fact that this atrocity did happen.

Acknowledging the existence in England of the problems they are experiencing, I must add at this point, perhaps that is the reason for the "National Defense Authorization Act." Certainly it is hopeful on my part that the intent is not to bring about martial law. *All* of any ethnic group cannot be bad but, the influence of some or many can be detrimental. Consider all of this article and ask yourself, if I were leading this country, how would I handle the situation? Perhaps one should take a lesson from the Australian government!

Fanaticism is always dangerous, and we must always be on the alert for what history has taught us.

E-mail Sent to
Congressman Rooney

I am kind of perplexed and would like some clarity. Let me try to have you understand why I am perplexed.

It appears the Republican Party wants to cut $61 billion from the federal budget. This amount seems to be what they want, to avert a shutdown of our government. It seems to me, I remember, for the middle class and lower class to maintain their tax break, the upper 2 percent would have to be allowed their break totaling $700 billion or the Republicans would not allow the unemployment checks, etc. to benefit the middle—and lower-class people, and they also would not be allowed the tax break that was established by G. W. Bush. How can I separate out the fact that this is a win-win situation only for the rich and to hell with the middle class and the poor because that is where you are looking to cut the budget. Seems pretty sick to me!

How can you justify the top four hundred people in the chain of wealth have more wealth than the lower 150 million people?

This is the response I got on April 6, 2011:

From: Representative Tom Rooney <FL16TRIMA@ mail.house.gov>
Subject: Responding to your message
To: perscoment@yahoo.com
Date: Wednesday, April 6, 2011, 6:36 PM

Dear Mr. Gardner:

Thank you for taking the time to contact me. I appreciate hearing your concerns and welcome the opportunity to respond.

As you may know, the 111th Congress failed to pass a budget for fiscal year 2011, leaving all functions of the federal government to be funded by a series of continuing resolutions. On February 19, the House of Representatives passed a continuing resolution to fund the federal government through September 30th. This CR contained $61 billion in spending cuts across the board. Unfortunately, the majority in the Senate rejected this long-term CR, forcing the House to choose between a series of short term continuing resolutions or allowing the government to shut down.

A government shutdown is not a viable option and would be seriously detrimental to our entire economy. We simply cannot play politics and allow our troops to fight a war without pay or allow seniors to have a lapse in the social security payments. The reality of the situation is that if Congress does not make tough choices now, both the prosperity of our nation and our national security will be seriously compromised. The federal government must join the American people, get our nation back on track, and begin to cut our crippling deficit. I am hopeful that we will come to an agreement to fund the remainder of this Fiscal Year so Congress can begin to debate and work through our budget plan for next year.

Please know that I will do everything in my power to ensure that our government remains funded, and that a full-year budget is passed. The continuing resolution is just the beginning of many more tough choices ahead. I am committed to working with my colleagues to develop a sustainable, responsible budget, while avoiding a government shutdown. While we may not agree on every issue, please know that implementing policies that will stimulate the economy, create jobs, and change our nation's fiscal path is my top priority in Congress.

I always appreciate hearing my constituents' opinions, especially on such an important issue. Thank you again for contacting me and please do so in the future if I may be of assistance.

Sincerely,

Thomas J. Rooney
Member of Congress

Now I ask you, did I get an answer to my question or just double talk?

So I wrote back:

Dear Representative Rooney,

For whatever reason, you have completely disregarded my question as to why the Republican Party refused to allow the rescission of the tax reduction for the upper income class that would have amounted to $700 billion. A recession that was rejected while the middle class and lower income class would have needed that reduction for their very survival. The rich wouldn't have even felt the loss. It seems ludicrous when you consider you are about to shut down the government for a few billion dollars when you could have had $700 billion to help reduce the deficit. I want you to explain that issue more than any other.

Somehow, I just can't seem to understand why it was so difficult for a supposedly educated man to understand my question. The middle class was about to lose their unemployment benefits if the rich couldn't keep their tax break. Somehow, I cannot seem to understand, if the government was out of funds and they could get $700 billion from the wealthiest people, which wouldn't hurt them at all, why was the middle class and lower class kept hostage?

It seems to me the Democrats were threatened, and no one saw it. The middle class and the lower class needed that tax break, while the wealthiest would find it to be just like a mosquito. Something bothersome but not difficult to swat.

Ratified Amendments to the Constitution[1]

1st Protects the freedom of speech, freedom of religion, and freedom of the press, as well as the right to assemble and petition the government.

2nd Protects an individual's right to bear arms. The origination of this amendment was to allow the people to protect themselves from the government.

3rd Prohibits the forced quartering of soldiers out of war time. Somehow, I think this amendment is a little outdated.

4th Prohibits unreasonable searches and seizures and sets out requirements for search warrants based on probable cause.

5th Sets out rules for indictment by grand jury and eminent domain, protects the right to due process, and prohibits self-incrimination and double jeopardy.

6th Protects the right to a fair and speedy public trial by jury, including the rights to be notified of the accusations, to confront the accuser, to obtain witnesses, and to retain counsel.

7th Provides for the right to trial by jury in certain civil cases, according to common law.

---

[1]   From Wikipedia

8th Prohibits excessive fines and excessive bail, as well as cruel and unusual punishment.

9th Protects rights not enumerated in the constitution.

10th Limits the powers of the federal government to those delegated to it by the constitution.

12th Revises presidential election procedures.

13th Abolishes slavery and involuntary servitude, except as punishment for a crime

14th Defines citizenship, contains the Privileges and Immunities Clause, the Due Process Clause, and the Equal Protection Clause, and deals with post-Civil War issues.

15th Prohibits the denial of suffrage based on race, color, or previous condition of servitude.

16th Allows the federal government to collect income tax.

17th Establishes the direct election of United States Senators by popular vote.

18th Establishes prohibition of alcohol (*repealed by twenty-first amendment*)

19th Establishes women's suffrage.

20th Fixes the dates of term commencements for Congress (January 3) and the president (January 20); known as the "lame-duck amendment."

21st Repeals the eighteenth amendment.

22nd Limits the president to two terms, or a maximum of ten years (*i.e., if a vice president serves not more than half of a president's term, he or she can be elected to a further two terms*).

23rd Provides for representation of Washington, D.C. in the Electoral College.

24th Prohibits the revocation of voting rights due to the non-payment of poll taxes.

25th Codifies the Tyler Precedent; defines the process of presidential succession.

26th Establishes the official voting age to be eighteen years old.

27th Prevents laws affecting Congressional salary from taking effect until the beginning of the next session of Congress.

And the 28th Amendment, not yet ratified, is as follows:

<u>28th Amendment</u>

"Congress shall make no law that applies to the citizens of the United States that does not apply equally to the Senators or Representatives;

And Congress shall make no law that applies to the Senators or Representatives that does not apply equally to the citizens of the United States ."

"Before an amendment can take effect, it must be proposed to the states by a two-thirds vote of both houses of Congress or by a convention called by two-thirds of the states, and ratified by three-fourths of the states or by three-fourths of conventions thereof, the method of ratification being determined by Congress at the time of proposal.

"To date, no convention for proposing amendments has been called by the states and only once—in 1933 for the ratification of the twenty-first amendment—has the convention method of ratification been employed."[2]

---

[2]   From Wikipedia

Washington's Political War.

Perspicacity at its most ignorant moment; what is right is not necessarily *politically correct!* Written November 2011:

President Barack Obama

As the negotiations continue and the president continues to give in to the demands of the Republicans of the House, I want all to maintain the reasons he is doing this and sacrificing his position in politics.

Barack Obama didn't create the problems we have today, such as two wars, failing banks and insurance companies, an economy that is on the brink of disaster, and a worldwide collapse of the banking system. He inherited all this from a child before him. When G. W. Bush was appointed president of the United States, at that very moment, I proclaimed we would be at war with Iraq within two years.

When President Clinton signed into law the NAFTA set up by Ronald Reagan, I said we would lose many of our factories and there would be economic chaos.

I am not the most brilliant, educated individual on the face of the earth, but all this was just so obvious I couldn't comprehend why no one else saw it.

Why do you think we attacked a sovereign nation that never provoked us? Oh yes, they supposedly had weapons of mass destruction. We had the United Nations investigating that charge, and in a very short time, their report would have come back as; that accusation was completely false, for the only weapons of mass destruction Saddam had were the nerve gas bombs we gave to him when he was at war with Iran. I believe that President Bush and Vice President Cheney saw an opportunity and seized it. G. W. Bush wanted revenge on Saddam for trying to kill his father, and Dick Cheney wanted the oil. I believe that and cannot understand why charges were never brought against them for it.

If you remember, during the presidential campaign, Senator McCain had to leave the campaign trail and go to Washington because AIG was about to go under, bringing with them the banking system. The really sad part of this is that AIG used the funds, as I understand, to give executive bonuses to the executives who brought AIG to the point of failure. An executive bonus should only be paid when a company is successful and draws a profit.

Barack Obama was running for office of the presidency. He was not president yet, so blaming him cannot be correct. He did, however, avert a calamity of unparalleled proportion and has taken the fall for something he never created. Now he is trying to hold the line for the mistakes made and at the end of this critique, I will give my analysis of how to properly correct the problem, which is a little of give and take.

House Speaker John Boehner

As the political war goes on and on, to do what is expedient seems to be overpowered by the political ambition to place blame. It certainly seems neither party gets things right because they do not wish to get things right. Each must put enough blame on the other to create a political landslide come election time. Dividing the country is the name of the game here.

On August 8, 2010 on "Meet The Press," John Boehner showed the world that he didn't understand what a question was. When asked, three separate times, if the tax cuts were paid for, he repeatedly skirted the question. He said we need to get more money in the hands of small businesses and American families to get our economy going again. Since that time, he has threatened that unless the super-rich and the extremely wealthy get to keep their tax cuts, fostered by that child that was in the White House, he would stop the unemployment checks and entitlements—thereby accomplishing nothing but to hurt the most vulnerable of our society. Here we go again! The working-class people who supported, defended, and gave much of their families' and friends' lives, once again, should shoulder the burden of the Washington screw-ups. He claims he was a small businessman before going to Washington, and this, of course, makes him an authority on how to fix the mess we are in. I do not see any plans to bolster the small business and American families.

The Three Branches of Government

I don't know about such things as to why Washington should be run like a business because it seems to me that a business needs to make profits, while government is supposed to serve the people. We all entrust those we elect to make our lives better than the former generation, but we certainly don't entrust them to create a society outside the laws of the rest of us. It sure seems strange to me that the men and women that defend and have defended this great nation are paid very little to put their lives on the line. If they manage to stay for a twenty-year term, they are given a pension of half the salary of the highest rank they achieved while in the service of their country. The representatives and senators need only stay in office six years while they are defended by those same people and they get 100 percent of what their salary was, plus expense accounts and a health program of insurance that is rivaled nowhere. Oh! Did I forget to mention their salary is just about $175,000 per year? Oh! Did I forget most if not all are multimillionaires today? In my opinion, not a one has ever read and understood the preamble to the Constitution, where it proclaims, " Secure the blessings of liberty to ourselves and our posterity." Posterity! Now that seems to be a peculiar word. Could it be our off spring? Oh well! Forget about that, because they care only for their own, as they want to destroy everyone else's.

I cannot help but wonder why, when I talk to people about politics, there seems to be only two types of people: Republicans and Democrats. The Democrats can't seem to agree on anything, while the Republicans hold strong as if they were hypnotized. I don't think you could get

100 percent of the Democrats to agree that two and two equal four! Well, perhaps there is a good side to that story. Perhaps they are doing their job, having individual opinions on subjects instead of being robots and not even formulating any opinions. A result of which, they are not really perspicacious to the fact that they aren't doing their job that we sent them to Washington to do.

Let's take away from Social Security and Medicare and Medicaid. Let's hurt the middle class in the pocketbook and never mind the veterans, because they have little or no way of defending themselves. While the major corporations making billions not only get away without paying their share but get subsidies from those hard-working Americans that make up the middle class and the poor. Strange how, after Katrina hit New Orleans, it left a stadium full of people without food and water for a week, while around the world disasters are attended to in a matter of two or three days. Somehow, I cannot fathom that.

I think it is time the American people began paying their fair share—based on their wealth and income. The present tax system stinks, and Washington knows it but won't do anything about it.

John Boehner, you want to reduce the federal government, and I agree it is too big under the present circumstances. Let's first agree on the fact that the United States of America is the greatest country in the world, but we can make it better.

First let's understand that those factories, approximately fifty thousand of them, left this country over the last ten years. Let's understand that they left here because they were given substantial incentives to do this. Let's understand that as long as it is profitable for them to operate outside the USA, we will not have any factories. Since we have little to no factories creating jobs, there will be little to no people that can afford to purchase those items they are manufacturing and therefore there is a stalemate.

Now, let's thwart that idea by creating an import tax that is realistic. After all, the power to levy import taxes was created by our forefathers to protect our jobs. China has a 22 percent import tax, Pakistan has a 40 percent import tax, and we have a 2 percent import tax. If the other countries don't like it, tell them where to get off, as we must take care of our own first.

For what reason do we have over a thousand military installations in some 139 countries? This country is supposed to be a republic, but it sure seems to me that it is an empire. We have floating cities called aircraft carriers that can go to any point in the world if needed; we don't need those military installations so we can dictate to the world how to run their countries. Hell, we can't even run our own country. We have the most powerful weapons on the face of the earth, known as nuclear submarines, and between those aircraft carriers and nuclear submarines, why would we need bases all over the world?

In the 1960s, we proved to the world that we could have any number of troops sent to any point in the world inside of seventy-two hours. Now we have super-transport aircraft, such as the C-5A, for just those occasions. The *eye* of the world in space can see any point in the world where unrest occurs. We do not need to be where we are not welcome, and we certainly do not need the expense. Start by changing that and not jumping on a sound system of entitlements.

If you really want to begin reducing the deficit, how about working for free, as our forefathers did in the beginning! Let's cut out some of those perks and see how long you continue to work as a representative of the people. Four hundred and five people in Congress drawing at least $175,000 per year totals more than $70 million. Now that would be a good start to reduce the deficit. How about no longer subsidizing the oil companies? Since there is only one country that appreciates us, how about stopping the outflow of donations by this government to other countries? Since the name of the game is profit, how about we stop subsidizing the drug companies, as they can do pretty well on their own? Strange how we can buy drugs from Canada a lot cheaper than we can buy them here, where supposedly we manufacture them.

How about diverting some of those subsidies over to our teachers to insure a competitive level of education with the rest of the world? How about stopping the influx of foreign people that we are subsidizing while our people suffer? How about just giving a damn about the future of this nation instead of what is politically expedient? Please don't tell me that having a universal health plan would bankrupt this nation. We are the only industrialized nation on the planet without one. The US government can't stop the fraud in Medicare, but the Medicare Advantage Plans can. Does that tell you something? Let's get the US government out of everyone's business and out of our homes. The government was never intended to tell us how to raise our children. Sure, there will be children subject to abuse, but that is not for the US government to legislate. Some children will suffer, but the majority will most likely benefit. There is a shortage of discipline within the confines of the family, and you are the reason for it.

Now let's get to the real destroyer of this national monetary crisis: The inept attitude of the legal system. Soon we will have more people in prison than out. You take a young person that becomes a victim of a small-time drug dealer, partly because they are given no discipline at home because the government is in their house. You convict that young person of a nonviolent crime and tag them with a title known as a felon. Maybe your judges put them in rehabilitation for one or two years. Now they get out but are on probation. This same person now cannot get a job because they are felons and you expect them to starve. Without the ability to get a job, they must turn to the only people that will give them a job, and that is selling drugs or prostitution—both of which are illegal. This serves two purposes. It increases the field force for the drug cartels along with increasing their bottom line and subtracting it from ours. The drug lords won't pay any taxes. And, it feeds the prison lobby people, as we are constantly in need of more space to teach these violators a lesson so when they get out they can create more violators and we will need more prisons. I wonder, what percentage of these small-time violators becomes rehabilitated and stay out of our prison system. Please pardon my opinion, but that is the dumbest thing anyone could possibly do, and it starts with the stupidity of Washington taking its finger off the pulse where it should be. You stick your noses where they do not belong but refuse to see the forest for the trees.

The United States government has specific duties, which are clearly laid out in the Constitution. Try giving a shit about the people! Raise the debt ceiling and then begin to bring the U.S. government under control. You are servants of the people, not the other way around.

End the programs that are fat and build up the meat of the concept.

Promote the general welfare. I am sure there is plenty of funds to keep the promise of Social Security if you would just keep your hands off of the funds and distribute them to what they were meant for.

Promote the universal health plan so we can get a hold of the inflationary spiral the medical and pharmaceutical industries have been creating.

Promote education so that we can keep the promise to the people of *No Child Left Behind.*

Raise the import taxes to generate more funds as well as bring back our factories i.e., jobs.

Change the present tax structure so that it is fair and equitable.

Defend this nation, not the rest of the world. We have more natural resources than any other nation, and we have the greatest people on the planet, as we are made up of a diversity of ethnic and international people. For a while, we will need to develop a system of isolationism from the rest of the world in order to bolster our nation, and we can do it, but the entire nation must be behind it for if we are not, we will surely fail, and your pensions and medical insurance and perks won't be worth spit.

This is the *United States of America*. We must stand united for the betterment of this most wonderful nation and not for the benefit or control of those few refusing to do their job. You have a job, and if you can't do it, get the hell out of office and let people in that do want to do it. By the way, we seem so impressed with the education of our leaders, but let me remind you that one of the greatest presidents ever, only had a high school diploma and one of the worst bought his degree.

The above statements are the opinion of one person: me. If my opinion stands and other people concur with it, then it will be the opinion of many and soon the entire nation will see the need for reform. The preamble begins with *"We the people."* Let's not forget that!

Our President: What the Hell Is He Thinking?

For the first time in my life, I have a prediction that frightens me to the extreme point such as I have never been frightened before. I received an e-mail from a dear friend of mine that is so twisted it has made me realize we as a nation are in more trouble than anything imaginable.

The title above, as it was presented, is to indicate that Barack Obama has awarded contracts to the Chinese people to rebuild America's infrastructure. According to the e-mail, the story was presented on ABC news. I watched the report as presented by the e-mail and what it showed was President Obama telling the people:

"Help us rebuild this bridge."

"Help us rebuild America."

"Help us put Americas construction workers back to work."

The next thing was an insinuation that Barack Obama was hiring Chinese contractors to rebuild America's infrastructure and cutting out the American workers.

I cannot believe my eyes and ears as to how low some people can go to stoop down and defame anyone under such false pretenses. I began to realize there is more to this than just defaming an American president. There is a direct attempt to undermine the entire country. The world is at stake here and it is directed to the Republican Party that I make this prediction.

In New York, a $400,000 renovation of a bridge known as the Alexander Hamilton Bridge; in California, a $7.2 billion bridge to connect San Francisco and Oakland; in Alaska, a $190 million bridge project are all to be constructed. Sounds like a great opportunity for government spending to lead to real jobs. Wow! But the problem is much of the work is going to Chinese government-owned contracting firms.

Scott Paul, of the Alliance for American Manufacturing, as well as unions are pushed to an obvious point. "This is not the time to send more jobs to China. Our tax dollars should provide hundreds of jobs for Americans. US law requires major infrastructure jobs to be done by Americans if the cost is reasonable. In California, US firms said they would meet these guidelines. *Their officials decided to turn down federal money for the bridge, allowing a Chinese company to get the job at a cost of over three thousand American jobs and a cost potential of $1 billion boost for the American economy.*

Luis Alejo, a Democratic assemblyman, said this is not only jobs but spending that would have been reinvested back into our economy.

Tony Anziano of the California Department of Transportation said it is a struggle to obtain welders, which is his excuse. When asked if they have done everything possible to keep jobs here, he said, "Absolutely."

Tell me another one, I will just believe anything you tell me because it must be the truth. I can't imagine any reason for someone to give out a contract to an overseas contractor without some incentive. I guess you are just interested in saving the USA some money!

My reply to my friend was as follows:

Here we go again! Did you see or hear one word from Obama about sending the contracts to China to rebuild our bridges? Go to ABCnews.com and this is what you will see:

> In California, *officials* actually claimed that American companies simply could not do the work as fast or as cheap, yet multiple US firms have stated that they would have gladly provided the workers.

> Sadly, many in the corporate-controlled media are merely pretending to care about the destruction of America and, for the most part, have literally worshiped globalism.

(I didn't write this; look and see for yourself—all I did was copy and paste.)

This is a plot to seed your mind. Go there and see for yourself, I am not lying or rewriting the information. No one blamed Obama from the news; in fact his name didn't even come up. *Subversive propaganda,* that is what you are getting. The major corporations are out to rule the world, and people such as those that put Obama's name on this are spreading propaganda and making you believe it but see for yourself, it isn't true.

The Supreme Court opened the door for unlimited funds to be invested in an election, and in my opinion, the Chinese people are taking great advantage of that ruling. The major corporations of this country are sending the jobs to the owned corporations in China and the American middle class is going to be crushed.

Now for my promised predictions:

Eventually the American people will be pushed to the limits and will rebel. When that happens, one of the other countries, such as China or Russia, will be able to step in and take us over. At that moment, this nation, which has been the greatest nation on Earth, will be destroyed. Our defenses will be no longer, and our economy will also be no longer. We will become what we have always turned against: slaves in a country that is dominated by a communist regime. Our only defense may be that this country has the largest and most dangerous guerilla army the world has ever known, thanks to the Second Amendment to our constitution. Do not forget in the 30s, 40s, and 50s what happened with the unions in this country. Please never forget that! *History repeats itself, and those that refuse to learn from it are doomed to relive it.*

You will see killing of Chinese workers by sniper fire and destruction of completed work in an effort to undermine the contracts. I cannot imagine the people accepting that we, the greatest building nation ever, are not capable of building the infrastructure of our country. We have built the greatest structures, the Empire State Building, The greatest art deco in the world in the Chrysler building, the twin towers, bridges, tunnels, the most complex rail system in the world, subways, dams, defense mechanisms, ships, underground facilities, aquariums, and I could go on all day. Are we ready to accept that we cannot supply accomplished welders as a reason for subbing out our infrastructure?

Are we so ready to blame a man of color with a funny name that goads us into a frenzy that, he is a Muslim which he is not? Are you ready to accept that such a man who has:

Averted a depression
Saved the American auto industry
Got healthcare passed
Wall Street reform
Consumer Protection Bureau
Student loan and credit card reform
Troops out of Iraq
Don't Ask Don't Tell
Two women on the Supreme Court.
Downed Osama Bin Laden, Anwar al-Awlaki, Atiyah
    Abd al-Rahman, and Muammar Gaddafi (Qaddafi)
    truly is evil and wants only to destroy this nation?

What does it take to remember the people wanted to stone Moses for his failures in their stupidity and disappointment? NAFTA sent our factories away, creating the great unemployment, not Obama. A child in the White House created two wars, not Obama. And the Republican Party created the opening for these false but devastating mortgages and cannot run on its own merits, so they create an issue such as this and then connect our president to it when he had nothing to do with it. This president is guilty of only one thing: trying to get America back together again.

Difficult when you have an organization fighting you all the way in an effort to regain power in the White House and thus bring about our destruction; to reverse all that has been done in the name of the *people*! Difficult when you have an organization using their own morals to strip away the rights that women have regarding their health and welfare. In the year 2000, my son advised that the fix was in and as a Republican I couldn't see it then, until I saw the famous butterfly ballot, and it was then that I knew he was right. It was then when the Supreme Court appointed G. W. Bush that I knew and stated, "We will be at war with Iraq within two years." I only have one question for the people. When someone holds 98 percent of the people hostage for the benefit of 2 percent of the people, how can you still hold true to those people? I do not think I will ever be able to accept that form of logic.

Wake up America before it is too late!

Change must be made, but destruction is all that I can see!

Epilogue

There is very little anyone of us can do, as the government has taken over and they are controlled by *big money*! The people, as I have seen by the advertisements, are being led by the nose and are actually hypnotized.

The unaccountable lies that are being told and those that want to believe tell me that this free nation is losing ground.

Our politicians have only one goal and that is power. They refuse to realize there is something bigger, and when that something bigger fails their power will also be destroyed. They could have made a difference and will someday regret they didn't.

Our legal system is unbelievable, as the prosecutors are more interested in winning than getting to the truth. Please keep in mind that the prosecutor is also immune to prosecution, even for withholding exculpatory information, protected by none other than the Supreme Court.

Our judges fail to realize it is the system that should be put on trial, not the victims. Most of the drug addicts are victims, not criminals, but they are treated as criminals, while the real criminals are free to perpetuate the victimization.

The prison lobbyists are having a financial field day, a disease we cannot afford to perpetuate. Our jails take in people the judges send to them and, instead of feeding them proper food, give them food they cannot stomach while charging them for each day. Now, how do they expect them to pay? They are incarcerated! That food is paid for by the taxpayers; why are the prisoners being charged, and why isn't the health department checking for the bugs that are in the food?

The prisons are making a fortune on phone calls, as the calls are free but not to the people on the outside who are expecting to speak with their loved ones. Those people must deposit funds in order to receive a phone call, and they are charged just for the privilege of making that deposit.

It is almost impossible to get medical assistance; even the most basic needs are ignored.

Freedom has been eroded each and every time new legislation is passed. The banks are having a field day, as they refuse to negotiate with the homeowners, and the homeowners are telling the banks where to get off. Soon the banks will own unbelievable numbers of vacant homes and be forced to pay maintenance and taxes for each. They will settle on short sales, which is quite a bit less than the actual devalued value, as an alternative to negotiating with the people holding the mortgage. They think the government will make up the difference, but they fail to realize the government is also broke. Where does it end?

Stupidity! How about the *oil* that we are paying so dearly for? Common sense should tell that you cannot keep taking from the Earth and expect that nothing will happen. For every action, there is an equal and opposite reaction. I am not a scientist, but it is pretty obvious to me that oil is the hydraulic fluid that fills in the imperfections in the structure of the Earth, and soon the very shape of this planet will change from round to whatever. When that happens, the earth will be thrown off its axis, and we will all broil or freeze to death. Perhaps not in our lifetime, but doesn't anyone have thoughts for their grandchildren? Our transportation is dependent on oil by design for greed purposes.

Why do we not have monorails throughout the country that are run by renewable electric energy? The horse and buggy days ended, and so should this era of the internal combustion engine.

Why not do away with the *tax breaks and subsidies* given to the oil companies and use the funds to create monorail systems and in so doing create employment and perhaps even save the planet? Save our economy at the very least!

I am sorry for the length of this article, but I am so frustrated with the lack of consideration for our fellow man and at the same time our posterity. This is the greatest country ever in the history of the world but we *will* destroy it soon if we do not start respecting our planet and our fellow human beings. A result of our superior intellect, we are the gatekeepers of this planet, but we aren't showing very much intellect when we hunt species to extinction, pollute our waterways and the air we breathe, and completely ignore Mother Nature. Perhaps it is time for Klaatu, because I do not see us changing and our leaders will not wake up.

We the people are not responsible for our actions after being spoon-fed lies and deceit and twisted facts, all in the name of power. The politicians are all talking about the national debt. Funny, but back in the days when McGovern and Humphrey campaigned against one another, they said the exact same things Romney is saying today. Look back and see that I am correct. The only one who did something about the budget by turning over a balanced one was Clinton—and guess what the child after him did!

Religious Freedom!

Wow, now that is the biggest problem of all. Every person is entitled to believe the way they wish except those that do not believe the way I want them to! Where is the logic in the fact that religion has been the leading factor in violent death? I find it hard to understand how the religious preference which I accept is in any way harmful or dangerous to anyone else. Why do you find my thoughts and practices intolerable just because they are not congruent with yours? I find it almost inconceivable that so many Christians I have conversed with have no idea that Christ was born a Jew and died a Jew. In fact, he was a rabbi! How can they love one man so much and hate all his people? Why is it that to some religions it is suggested they kill all other religions? I was of the belief that religion taught good things to shape the way for people to live in harmony not *hate*! The teachings of morals and respect toward life. To set the record straight, I do not practice any religion, as I am a self-proclaimed agnostic. I was born into a Jewish family but do not take the philosophies as a science. I believe if there is a God, let him show himself to all of us and tell us all how to live our lives because we obviously are all lost.

The very idea that man was given dominion over the earth (because of his will and intellect) very obviously is an obtuse idea, as we obviously are incongruent with our neighbors and our environment. We hate and fear because those that wish power tell us to, and it is by our very nature tantamount to be right even when we are wrong. Does there always have to be a right and wrong?

Through education, logic and maturity, we find that many of the teachings of our ancestors were incorrect but the leaders of our faith tell us we must continue to believe those antiquated ideas. Do you still listen to your father who tells you to prepare food the way the ancient people did? That idea is absurd; we know better today and that thought was false. Old ideas, such as "don't drive a car on the Sabbath to a house of worship," should be thrown out, as it was only to give the beast of burden a day of rest. Well guess what? That car couldn't care less if it was Sabbath or Wednesday. Even though 98 percent of Catholic women contribute to the drug system by using birth control, they are told it is against the religion.

People have forgotten about women dying in back alleys after having an abortion from an unqualified person using a wire hanger in a totally unsterile environment. I mentioned this in the chapter "Free Country." The very arrogance of one party to try to force their will, their beliefs, on us, to me, is absurd to say the least. Politicians are not put in a position of decision to change my religious or personal beliefs! You may still believe in witchcraft and burning of witches, but don't try to make me believe your way. This is supposed to be a free country, one where free thinking is supposed to be allowed—not stifled by the morals of another. Don't tell me how to believe! What makes you so right that you cannot withstand the possibility that you are not? Your morals and ideas are yours, and I'll thank you to keep them to yourself. I find your overbearing desire to rule my mind repugnant and intrusive. Your job is to take care of the business of the nation, not to tell me how to live my personal life and certainly not to impose your beliefs on me or anyone else in this great nation. We are here because we are free. We haven't hired you to take that away from us.

There are many rules that are no longer correct yet people, caught up in the grips of fear, still follow them and will defend to the death if necessary what they were told as children by people not capable of seeing the truth. You want a religion that makes sense? I'll give one to you! Love thy neighbor, and try not to hurt anyone. Respect the planet and all that God has given to you. Learn to better life through technology, and stop letting people tell you to hate any other people! Simple huh? You don't need any priest, rabbi, minister, or any other religious leader to tell you that; it is written in the book of common sense.

We have so many different kinds of people, just as we have so many different species of animals or plants. All the people have the same thoughts: live in freedom, help the needy, and hope our children become the best people they can become.

We have men, women, gays, lesbians, Caucasians, Blacks, Indians, Asians, Brown people, people of no color at all, people of so many religions, I couldn't even begin to list them—nor should I try.

Such grand diversity, separated only by thoughts of dominance and fear of perpetuation loss. All have brains, feelings, desires, and wants. All want the same things but kept apart by *hate* and *fear*.

Let's break that chain and try to live together. Our diversity is what makes us great and we are all part of the same *race*. We are all human beings with the same need to nurture and be nurtured. Throw away that ignorance and try to help those that need the help. *be a good neighbor*!

If believing the way you choose brings you peace of mind, how wrong could it be, and why should someone else tell you your thoughts are wrong? Think my way! As long as you aren't interfering with everyone else's lives, do whatever you feel works for you!

In today's way of life, with technology being the basis for our daily lives, lying is almost impossible, and living a lie is getting more and more complicated. Stop listening to and accepting the lies that are being told to you, and do not give in to fear.

We are in a changing world. History has taught us much, and we must learn about it or we will return to the days of the dictator. We will return to the days of tyranny and insecurity. We must all try to live in harmony and not judge others for their beliefs different than ours.

We, the people of the United States, must lead by example. We cannot make a very good impression when we are so divided. We can make this country great again and lead by example and deed. Power can only protect us so we can make this world a better place to live for all.

If I have opened anyone's mind and hearts by what I have articulated here, and I can leave one thought that remains constant in your mind, please, before you get all in a huff over what you have heard, be it on the Internet or TV or radio or perhaps from a friend or relative. Do not, and I repeat, do not draw any conclusions without first checking out the validity of the statement. I think you will find that almost all of the items that impose fear are false. Live by knowledge of the truth and dispel the lies. You will be much calmer and happier for it.

Martin L. Gardner

Definitions

Capitalism: Possession of capital; a system under which the production and distribution of goods and services are privately managed; *free enterprise.*

Capital: Any form of wealth employed for the production of more wealth; the wealth thus employed by a business or industrial or commercial enterprise which can be in the form of manufactured goods, money, stocks or bonds, or relatively permanent assets as machinery or buildings. In short, *wealth to produce more wealth.*

Democracy: demos = people; crat = rule.

Government by the people; a form of government in which the supreme power is vested in the people and exercised by them or their elected agents; a state having such a form of government; in a restricted sense, a state in which the supreme power is vested in the people and exercised directly by them rather than by their elected representatives; a state of society characterized by nominal equality of rights and privileges; political or social equality; democratic spirit; the common people of a community as distinguished from any privileged class; the common people with respect to their political power.

Republic: Res = an affair, interest; publica, fem. of publicus, public.

A state or other political unit in which the supreme power is vested in the whole voting community which elects, indirectly or directly, representatives to exercise the power; any group of persons with a common cause.

The United States of America is a republic that uses a democratic form of government! It is a terrible form of government, but I feel sure it is the best form of government on the planet today. It is my sincerest hope that Washington straightens out and does right by the people. This nation must lead by example and hopefully bring about:

World Peace.

On 3 November 1949, President Harry Truman appeared in St. Paul, Minnesota, in conjunction with that state's Truman Day Celebration, and that evening he delivered an address on the subject of opposition to democratic efforts to promote the general welfare, stating (in part):

We know that there will be more prosperity for all if all groups have a fair share of the wealth of the country. We know that the country will achieve economic stability and progress only if the benefits of our production are widely distributed among all its citizens.

We believe that it is the federal government's obligation, *under the Constitution, to promote the general welfare* of all our people—and not just a privileged few. The policies we advocate are based on these convictions.

We maintain that farmers, like businessmen, should receive a fair price for the products they sell.

We maintain that workers are entitled to good wages and to equality of bargaining power with their employers.

We believe that cooperatives and small business should have a fair opportunity to achieve success, and should not be smothered by monopolies.

We hold that our great natural resources should be protected and developed for the benefit of all our people, and not exploited for private greed.

We believe that old people and the disabled should have an assured income to keep them from being dependent on charity.

We believe that families should have protection against loss of income resulting from accident, illness, or unemployment.

We hold that our citizens should have decent housing at prices they can afford to pay.

We believe in assuring educational opportunities for all our young people in order that we may have an enlightened citizenry.

We believe in better health and medical care for everyone, not for just a few.

We hold that all Americans are entitled to equal rights and equal opportunities under the law, and to equal participation in our national life, free from fear and discrimination.

Acknowledgements and Resources

All my friends that gave to me so willingly their opinions and thoughts.

Wikipedia

CBS News

Face the Nation

FC&S Bulletins.

HBO

Meet the Press

Michael Purcell, publisher of *Pineapple Post*

My wife, Joan

Rick Fleishman and Scott Lutwak, personal editors.

NBC News

None Dare Call it Treason

Rhoda Viccari, to whom I shall be eternally grateful for all the e-mails.

The Heritage guide to the Constitution

The Living Webster Encyclopedic Dictionary of the English Language.

Snopes.com

Yahoo Mail

About the Author

Marty Gardner was born in 1942. Marty is a veteran of the United States Air Force, having served for four years. He comes from a home where the value of impression was more important than the quality of family. Through relations with his wife, Joan, and her family, he has learned the reverse.

Marty has a brother whom he is extremely proud of. His struggle to put himself through college and dental school displayed courage and strength of will that deserve admiration. Marty has a wife and three children: a son from his first marriage and two daughters from his second marriage. He also has three wonderful grandchildren, one boy and two girls. Poetic justice perhaps!

In 1965, Marty began his career in the insurance industry as an insurance consultant for Metropolitan Life Insurance Company. After Marty qualified for the life and health license, the realization that this would be the career he had been seeking emerged. Marty was now in a position to help people and earn a living at the same time, all while maintaining an aura of professionalism.

Since then, after moving to Florida and becoming independent, he completed courses and qualified for a license as a property and casualty insurance agent as well as qualifying to be a licensed adjuster. Caught somewhere in the middle of all this, in 1987, Marty earned a BBA degree. A native of Long Island New York, he has spent the last forty-two years in Florida.

Marty likes to listen to people express themselves, and he writes down much of what he hears so that he can check out the facts or fictions as an afterthought. He is very much a patriot and loves this country. He has expressed a deep concern for the manufactured lies told on the Internet, spread from one person to another without verification. He has received literally hundreds of false e-mails attempting to create fear by stretching the truth or manufacturing complete falsehoods, manipulating ideas to create fear in the hearts of the people. One of those lies states that a great source of truth, a place where one can always go to verify a rumor, is biased or under the monetary control of a particular philanthropist referred to as a communist. Some people are so afraid of the truth they create false rumors. That source is snopes.com, and if you will go to snopes.com and bring up Snopes in the subject bar, they will even tell you about this rumor. Both the rumor and the information are unjustifiable.

Should anyone be interested, Marty's favorite book is *None Dare Call It Treason* by John A. Stormer. It is his fondest wish that everyone read this book, as well as the sequel, *None Dare Call it Treason: The Next 25 Years*. When my father-in-law gave the first book to me, he told me it was suppressed by the US government originally. I do not know that to be a fact, but I can see why that might be true. History is a funny thing; although most do not like studying it in high school, as one ages, one often wants to learn more about it. There is an old saying:

"Those who refuse to learn from history are doomed to live it again."

No truer words have ever been spoken!

*9 7 8 1 4 7 7 2 8 0 5 6 0 *